WORLD CLASS CUISINE OF ITALY AND FRANCE

Special Thanks to

Berlitz International, Inc.
Ceramiche Rampini
Grey Poupon
Maison du Cadeau
Schieffelin & Somerset Co.

Other Books by Gail Greco

Country Inn Cooking
Great Cooking with Country Inn Chefs
The Romance of Country Inns
Tea-Time at the Inn
Secrets of Entertaining from America's Best Innkeepers
A Country Inn Breakfast
Bridal Shower Handbook
World Class Cuisine, 1993 and 1994 companion books

Companion book to the Discovery Channel's Premier Cooking Show

World Class Cuisine of ITALY AND FRANCE

Cooking with Recipes from the Provinces

GAIL GRECO

Photographs by Tom Bagley

RUTLEDGE HILL PRESS

Nashville, Tennessee

Created under the auspices of Arna Vodenos Productions (AVP),
131 Rollins Avenue, Suite 3, Rockville, Maryland 20852
as a companion book to the Discovery Channel television series *World Class Cuisine*.

The quotation on page *viii* is from *Songbirds, Truffles, and Wolves: An American Naturalist in Italy*,
by Gary Nabhan. Copyright 1993 by Gary Nabhan. Penguin Books USA Inc. Quotations on pages 3 and 37 are from *The Good Food of Italy*, by Claudia Roden. Copyright
1989, 1990 by Claudia Roden. Alfred A. Knopf, Inc. Quotations on pages 103 and 131
are from *Provence*, by Peter Mayle and Margaret Loxton. Copyright 1993 by Peter Mayle
and Margaret Loxton. Macmillan Publishing Co.

Published in Nashville, Tennessee, by Rutledge Hill Press, Inc.
211 Seventh Avenue North, Nashville, Tennessee 37219
Distributed in Canada by H. B. Fenn & Company, Ltd.,
1090 Lorimar Drive, Mississauga, Ontario L5S 1R7
Distributed in Australia by Millennium Books,
13/3 Maddox Street, Alexandria NSW 2015
Distributed in New Zealand by Tandem Press,
2 Rugby Road, Birkenhead, Auckland 10
Distributed in the United Kingdom by Verulam Publishing, Ltd.,
152a Park Street Lane, Park Street, St. Albans, Hertfordshire AL2 2AU

Book design by Bruce Gore/Gore Studio, Inc.
Cover photo by Tom Bagley
Photo Styling in Italy by Rita Calvert
Maps by Kathy White
Typesetting by D&T/Bailey Typesetting, Inc., Nashville, TN 37203

Library of Congress Cataloging-in-Publication Data

Greco, Gail.
    World class cuisine of Italy and France : cooking with recipes from the provinces /
Gail Greco : photographs by Tom Bagley.
        p.   cm.
    Includes index.
    ISBN 1-55853-362-1 (hardcover)
    1. Cookery, Italian   2. Cookery, French.   3. Restaurants—Italy—Guidebooks.
4. Restaurants—France—Guidebooks.   5. Italy—Guidebooks.   6. France—Guidebooks.   I. Title
TX723.G763 1995
641.5944—dc20   95-42893
                                                                                          CIP

Printed in the United States of America
1 2 3 4 5 6 7 8 9 — 00 99 98 97 96 95

Contents

For You, Angelina

It is no wonder that he waited for hours
at the crest of the hill for you to come walking up the street.
Even though the moon came out and went back in and came back out again, he waited.
"La luna splende per te," he sang. So many of us feel these words of passion toward you.
Indeed, the moon does shine for you, Mom. You are an angel, and the wait is
worth the phases of a millenium of moons if that is
what it takes to be with you again.

Bringing Home the Flavors of Two Great Culinary Nations

The recipes of Italy and France are vastly different, but they do have one thing in common: whether the dish is cooked over a flat-top stove or in a wood-burning oven, it will be delicious.

France and Italy are culinary leaders, and their food has been sought after and imitated all over the world. A discussion among food enthusiasts and professionals often leads to the question of which came first—Italian or French cuisine. Some say it was an Italian, not a Frenchman, who first elevated French cuisine to an art form. Who or what came first does not, really matter;

the worldwide reverence and respect for the cuisine of both nations cannot be denied.

As *World Class Cuisine* traveled Italy and France for its third season of bringing the flavor of Europe to television, it became apparent that art was actually the order of the day in both countries. Although the culinary styles of these two countries are very different, both emphasize basic country ingredients made into simple dishes with individual creative touches and incredibly orchestrated flavors. Both cuisines allow the genuine regional tastes of the people to shine through.

Sabrina Casagni offers up some fresh biscotti at Edy Bakery in Sinalunga, Italy.

Italy is always a wonderful place for me to visit because it is the home of my own family roots. As one chef pounds basil on an episode from Italy, I am reminded of images of my grandmother with her own marble mortar and pestle. The small trattorias or family restaurants we featured, reminded me of the Italian meals my ancestors brought over from the old country and I pondered many things, such as why my grandfather forgot to tell me of such warm and beautiful images as the macaroni vendors perched on the street corners, selling their fresh wares.

Flashes of my culinary past reminded me of the significance of something I read in Gary Paul Nabhan's book, *Songbirds, Truffles, and Wolves:*

"They sat patiently waiting on the hard wood benches of Ellis Island. Their faces reflected the nervousness they felt, but their eyes were shining with hope. Maria de Salla stood near a window, her arms stiffly pushing fists into the stretched pockets of her black coat. Within one of those clenched palms was the only bit of Italy she could take along; the seeds of a plum tomato that would guarantee decades of manicotti, lasagna, spaghetti marinara, and braciola.

"Kate Murphy sat in the front row, her arms encircling a blue-eyed toddler. At the bottom of her canvas sack on the floor were four seed potatoes, the same species that had survived the potato famine, traced back as far as family lore and human memory stretched. There were cabbage seeds in the lining of Karl Schmidt's suitcase, chile peppers in the band of Jose Sanchez's hat, and rye grains filled the toe of Ivan Ivanovich's

wool sock. These brand new Americans brought along these grains of life that gave them the confidence to start life anew in a strange land."

I have fond memories, too, of French cooking during my early childhood. My best friend in grade school had a French mother who was a wonderful cook. I first tasted Brie in her Bronx, New York, kitchen at about age eight. I was charmed by the covered brown individual crockery pots into which my spoon ladled its first taste of onion soup au gratin. I can remember nights at my friend's house tasting Lyonnaise potatoes and all sorts of pot-au-feu and cherry clafouti. I heard stories of my friend's mother telling my own mother—a wonderful Italian cook—not to wash the mushrooms—long before it became so popular to do so. Nan Hoctor was a true French cook—I was lucky to have the best of both culinary worlds while growing up.

Going back to the roots of culinary America reinforces what I said earlier. This is not a competition over which cuisine is the better or the best. They have both survived and continue to evolve, meeting the challenges of all sorts of dietary concerns and coming out winners as you can see in the recipes that follow.

I now understand why I enjoy eating out and turning it into a ritual.

The aggressive aromas of these two countries are intoxicating. It seems that in Italy and France all roads literally lead to buying or tasting something for the table. Use this book as your own road map to magical tastes and, I hope, memorable times.

In Appreciation

The *World Class Cuisine* television series team joins me in thanking:

The people of **Berlitz International** for providing Italian and French language instruction to members of our team: Berlitz Director of Marketing **Patricia Sze** for the vision to make our partnership a reality; Public Relations Manager **Diane Dunay** for her tireless efforts in coordinating the partnership as well as for her sincere interest in and cheerleading for our work on both the cookbook and the television program; **François Longeiret,** director of Berlitz instruction in Rockville, Maryland, for arranging our Italian and French lessons; and of course, our instructors: **Luisa Jones** for Italian, and **Laurence Mirandon** for French.

Aura Reinhardt and **Jeff Pogash** of **Schieffelin & Somerset** for their continued support of our work once again this year in providing fine wines and spirits for the tasting segments of the television program and for recipes throughout the book. Also, **Patrick Morley-Fletcher** and the entire **Hennessy** group for hosting us so graciously in Cognac, France.

Romano Rampini and his entire family at the **Ceramiche Rampini** shop in Radda in Chianti for providing us with their sophisticated yet warm and inviting pottery

The World Class Cuisine *team for France on the Champs Elysées in Paris: (from left) cameraman Vance Heflin, executive producer Arna Vodenos, grip Jonathan Zurer, grip Polly Forster, cookbook photographer Tom Bagley, cameraman Rob Davidian, and executive food editor Rosemary Brodeur. The crew for Italy consisted of director Richard Schreier; producer Joe Martin; food stylist Rita Calvert; on cameras: Austin Steo, Sheila Smith, Rob Davidian and Vance Heflin; grip Jonathan Zurer; translator/grip Jason Kaplan; and cookbook photographer Tom Bagley.*

to enhance the cookbook photos throughout Italy as well as many of the television shows also in their homeland.

Grey Poupon, and Media Services Manager Carole Walker, for providing the television crew with ground transportation in Italy and France.

Cathy Gruget and her family at their Maison du Cadeau store in Cognac for providing us with elegant Limoges china for use in a number of the television episodes and cookbook pictures in France.

Publisher Larry Stone and the entire team at Rutledge Hill Press for another top-notch, professional job in producing the companion cookbook for the *World Class Cuisine* television series once again.

JoAnne Larson for assistance in translating several of the recipes from France.

A special thank you to Julia Scartozzoni for all her help on both the cookbook and the television program—not only at her lovely Castello di Spaltenna, but throughout Italy.

And the chefs and owners of all the restaurants we featured for sharing their many culinary talents with us, our viewers, and our readers in a wonderful spirit of cooperation and friendship.

Personal thanks from both me and cookbook photographer Tom Bagley go to all of the members of the *World Class Cuisine* team:

Executive producer Arna Vodenos for once again making the cookbook and the television series a reality.

A special thank you to Rita Calvert for helping with so many of the cookbook photographs while also working on the television show.

The television crew in Italy: director Richard Schreier; producer Joe Martin; food consultant Rita Calvert; videographers Austin Steo, Sheila Smith, Rob Davidian and Vance Heflin; grip Jonathan Zurer; and translator/grip Jason Kaplan.

The television crew in France: director Arna Vodenos; executive food editor Rosemary Brodeur; videographers Rob Davidian and Vance Heflin; grips Jonathan Zurer and Polly Forster.

And the team back in the studio in Rockville, Maryland: scriptwriter Tricia Conaty, who also worked on pre-production and helped with various sections of this cookbook; post-production supervisor Michael Chaparro, who also filled in as director temporarily in Italy; and everyone else at Arna Vodenos Productions.

WORLD CLASS CUISINE OF ITALY AND FRANCE

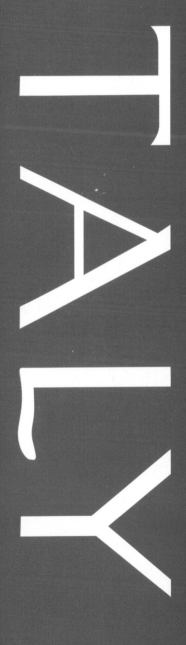

*It is easy to fall under the spell of Italy. . . .
Everyone can still be irresistibly charmed
by a country so full of natural beauty, art, music
and tradition; by a quality of life that warms the
heart and by food that is simple and unaffected but
full of rich flavors and delightful touches.*

Claudia Roden, *The Good Food of Italy*

ITALY

VALLE D'AOSTA

❦ ❦ ❦

Piedmont Province Produces Fabulous Fontina

*A*lthough it is Italy's tiniest region, Valle d'Aosta has made a giant contribution to the world by giving it Fontina cheese. A nutty-tasting cheese that is firm but creamy, Fontina is used in the cooking of Piedmont and the valley, especially in sauces and recipes for polenta. Fontina is often packaged in wheels weighing up to forty pounds, and ages as much as a hundred days before getting to the market.

The Piedmont area is nearly always associated with Valle d'Aosta because the fertile valley is a province of Piedmont. Bordered by Switzerland, Valle d'Aosta is dominated by the Alps. The area is an agricultural and dairy region with a cuisine that is simple but rich and hearty.

The alpine area is not only covered with chestnut trees that provide nuts, but also with wild game that put the likes of boar, deer, and mountain goat onto Piedmontese and Aostian tables. Pork sausages are another specialty because the sausages store well in winter months, when the growing season slows.

The region's high altitudes provide for an exceptional quality of butter. Potatoes, which are not the favored starch of Italy, are indeed the choice in Valle d'Aosta because they marry well with the strongly flavored dishes of this unique region.

Polenta is a staple of the area and it is not unusual to find ears of corn hanging to dry in great bunches in the sun to produce the cornmeal for polenta. Fruit grows in the hills so well that it has become the mainstay for Valle d'Aosta and Piedmont desserts from simple fruit tarts to pears with wine to strawberries with fresh, creamy cheese.

Corn, wheat, barley, rye, and oats are raised in the area's great plains, and between Piedmont and Valle d'Aosta some 60 percent of Italy's rice is produced.

Valle d'Aosta is one of the loveliest tourist areas of the Alps because of its dramatic vistas and contrasts. When traveling Italy, it may seem a hike to trek up to the smallest region, but the visit is like no other in the country and is a must-see.

Blue Lake and the Matterhorn

Dessert imitates art. (See page 8 for the sausage stew and Matterhorn cake recipes.)

- Preheat the oven to 450°. In a small saucepan, heat the olive oil over medium-high heat. When the oil is hot, add the rice and cinnamon and sauté for 2 minutes. Add 2 cups of the beef broth to the skillet, and place the mixture in the oven to bake in the pan for 20 minutes or until the rice is almost tender.
- Meanwhile, butter a 2-quart ovenproof soup ramekin. Fill the bowl half full with most of the bread slices. Top with most of the Fontina cheese and then the cooked rice. Sprinkle with the Parmesan cheese and add the remaining bread slices. Press down to make the mixture compact. Ladle enough broth to cover. Sprinkle with the remaining Fontina cheese. Bake 20 minutes or until browned and crispy on top.

YIELD: 4 SERVINGS

Neiges d'Antan

Cinnamon-and-Rice Fontina Cheese Soup

1	tablespoon olive oil
1	cup white rice
1	teaspoon cinnamon
4-6	cups beef broth
6-8	small hard rolls, thinly sliced
2	cups cubed Fontina cheese, ½-inch cubes
¼	cup grated Parmesan cheese

Neiges d'Antan

Baked Cabbage and Bread Pudding

Although rough, this hearty type of soup or pudding is also refined. The Valle d'Aosta signature cheese, Fontina, is used here and the culinarily superior Savoy cabbage also enhances the tremendous flavor of this special dish.

4	small hard rolls, sliced ¼-inch thick
¾	cup cubed Fontina cheese, plus ¼ cup, grated
¼-½	head Savoy cabbage, coarsely chopped
4	cups beef broth or bouillon

- Preheat the oven to 350°. Bring a medium saucepan of water to boil over high heat. Add the cabbage and cook until very tender. Meanwhile, grease a 1-quart ovenproof soup bowl with butter. Place half the bread slices into the bottom of the bowl. Add the Fontina cheese.
- Drain the cabbage and add it to the bowl. Sprinkle with the grated Fontina cheese. Layer the remaining bread slices on top of the cabbage and press down to make compact.
- Ladle the bouillon over all these ingredients. Place in the oven and bake 20 minutes or until brown and puffed.

YIELD: 2 SERVINGS

Neiges d'Antan

Pappardelle with Beef and Venison

2	tablespoons olive oil
1	clove garlic, minced
1	small onion, peeled and diced
2-3	small dried chilies
1	rib celery, thinly sliced
1	carrot, peeled and diced
1	tablespoon each: chopped fresh rosemary, basil, and sage
1	pound boneless beef rump, cut into ¼-inch cubes
1	pound venison stew meat, cut into ¼-inch cubes
1	16-ounce can crushed tomatoes
½	cup red wine
	Salt and pepper
1	pound pappardelle pasta

Wine Suggestion

RUFFINO

RISERVA DUCALE

Chianti Classico
DENOMINAZIONE DI ORIGINE CONTROLLATA E GARANTITA
Riserva

BOTTLED BY
I. L. RUFFINO
PONTASSIEVE · ITALIA · 516/FI

750 ml ℮   ALCOHOL 13% BY VOL

A richly textured wine of great complexity and finesse, Ruffino's Riserva Ducale Gold Label is a Chianti Classico Riserva that will enhance this classic pappardelle.

- Heat the olive oil in a large skillet over medium-high heat. When the oil is hot, turn down to medium heat and add the garlic, onion, chilies, celery, carrots, rosemary, basil, and sage. Stir occasionally, cooking until the vegetables are tender, about 10 minutes.
- Add the beef and the venison and stir well. Add the tomatoes, followed by the wine. Season all with salt and pepper. Turn the heat down to a simmer. Cover and cook for 2 hours, turning occasionally.
- When the meat is almost tender, boil a pot of water for the pasta. Cook the pappardelle just until tender. Drain and add to the skillet, tossing well to coat. Serve immediately.

YIELD: 4 SERVINGS

Sausage Stew with Polenta

1	gallon water
	Sea salt
1½	pounds yellow cornmeal
1	tablespoon olive oil
1	pound sweet Italian link sausage, cut into 2-inch pieces
1	small onion, finely chopped
1	clove garlic
1	cup dry red wine
1	16-ounce can crushed tomatoes
	Fresh sage

- Pour the water into a large nonstick frying pan with high sides. Add 1 tablespoon or so of the sea salt. Pour in the cornmeal, whisking it in continuously. Continue to cook for 1 hour over low heat, stirring often, until very thick and solid.
- Heat 1 tablespoon of the olive oil in a medium skillet over medium-high heat. When the oil is hot, add the sausage and sauté for about 10 minutes, tossing occasionally. Remove the sausage from the skillet and transfer it to a medium saucepan. Add the onion and garlic to the sausage and stir. Add the red wine and the tomatoes. Cook about 10 minutes to reduce.
- To serve, invert the polenta onto a cutting surface. It will be very thick but still soft. Cut the polenta into wedges, using a knife or string (the latter may make it easier to cut without spreading). Place the polenta in the bottom of a serving dish. Top with the sausage stew and serve. Garnish with fresh sage leaves.

YIELD: 6 SERVINGS

Riserva Ducale Traditional is an earthy, rich, and rustic wine that will work well with the flavors of the Sausage Stew with Polenta.

Neiges d'Antan

Matterhorn Chestnut-and-Meringue Cake

The inn Neiges d'Antan is situated near the Italian-Swiss border, within range of the famous Matterhorn mountain. This dessert, layered with puffy white meringues, like the snowcaps in the distance, is on the inn's menu as a toast to its natural environment.

4	egg whites
1	cup confectioners' sugar, plus 3 tablespoons

1½	cups dried whole chestnuts, soaked 12 hours in water
½	cup cocoa powder, plus more for garnish
1	cup heavy cream
1½	cups sugar
3	cups water
½	cup dark rum

- Preheat the oven to 200°. Line a baking sheet with parchment paper. In a large stainless steel bowl, whisk together the egg whites with 3 tablespoons of the confectioners' sugar. Beat until stiff peaks form (about 25 minutes). Transfer the egg white mixture into a pastry bag fitted with a star tip. Pipe out 1-inch-diameter rosettes onto the parchment. Bake 2 to 3 hours or until very dry and crisp, but not brown. Remove from the oven and set aside.
- Meanwhile, peel the soaked and softened chestnuts. Cover the nuts with water in a medium saucepan and bring them to a boil. Turn the heat down to a simmer and cook for 3 hours. When the chestnuts are tender throughout, drain them and place the nuts in a food processor. Grind almost to a paste and place in a bowl.
- Prepare a sugar syrup. In a small saucepan, boil the 1½ cups sugar and the water until thick. Add the syrup, along with the rum, to chestnuts in bowl. Sift in the cocoa, then stir into chestnut mixture. The mixture will be pastelike. Push the mixture through a ricer, sieve, or colander. The mixture will resemble coarse threads.
- Pour the threads out onto a serving plate in the shape of a mountain base (about 8 inches). Make a well in the center and fill with some of the meringues, like snow on top of the mountain.
- Whip the heavy cream with the remaining 1 cup of the confectioners' sugar. Place on top of the meringues. Keep building to make layers of meringues and whipped cream and sprinklings of cocoa powder until a mountaintop is formed. Sift cocoa over the top.

YIELD: 8 TO 10 SERVINGS

Neiges d'Antan

Fresh Fruit Aspic with Muscadet

The Loire Valley in France produces the sun-drenched white grapes for the light, dry Muscadet wine that seasons fresh fruit in this easy recipe.

¼	ounce gelatin
1	cup water
2	cups Muscadet wine
1	stick cinnamon
1	tablespoon black peppercorns
2	cups sugar
	Assorted fresh fruit (about 3 to 4 cups): kiwi, peaches, strawberries, and grapes, peeled and prepared and cut into bite-size pieces, plus more for garnish

- Soak the gelatin in the 1 cup of water to soften. Place the Muscadet in a medium saucepan with the cinnamon and peppercorns. Bring the mixture to a gentle boil, cooking over medium-high heat until the liquid is reduced by half, about 30 minutes. Add the sugar and mix in well. Add the softened gelatin. Remove the mixture from the heat and pass through a sieve, discarding the cinnamon stick and peppercorns. Cool until slightly thickened. Fill 8 small custard cups or ramekins halfway with fruit. Fill each cup with the aspic mixture and chill in the refrigerator until firm, at least 1 hour.
- To unmold, dip the bottom of each cup in a bowl of hot water for a few seconds to soften. Turn out onto individual serving plates. Ladle leftover aspic around foot of mold and add small bundles of fruit as garnish.

YIELD: 8 SERVINGS

LIGURIA

❦ ❦ ❦

Cuisine by the Sea with a Passion for Pesto

Stretching from the French border to
the foothills of Tuscany, the seaside towns
and villages that constitute Liguria's 200 or
so miles of sandy shores have contributed
foods that appear on the Italian menu
today. Oddly enough, seafood (while it
provides many of the raw ingredients to
Ligurian preparations) is not one of them.
Although some seafood is caught in its
waters, it is mostly shellfish and squid. The
Ligurians love pizza and top theirs with
anchovies, a tradition that has caught on
wherever pizza parlors exist.

There is further irony in that the Ligurian men, who voyaged at sea for months
at a time, greatly influenced Liguria's culinary character. But as you will see, seafood
specialties were not their contribution.
Actually, Liguria's culinary treasures come
from the terraced hillsides that scallop the
sea and produce vegetables in great abundance. A climate of brilliant, steady sunshine nurtures growth from even the tiny
crevices of stone walls where flowers cas-
cade and herbs grow madly.

*The pesto and pasta of Liguria as well as La Riserva's Apricot
Jellyroll Cake (see recipes on pages 13 and 16)*

The city of Genoa, perched right on
the crescent of this region, invented ravioli,
or in local dialect, *rabiole,* which translates as
leftovers that were enveloped in dough to
make a meal stretch. Ligurians are famous
for stuffing everything from meats and
shellfish to vegetables. Pasta of many styles
is of course another staple, and it is in Liguria where possibly the world's only
spaghetti museum exists. The region also
makes *farinate,* or soups with flours. But
what is perhaps most significant about Ligurian cuisine is its use of pesto sauce.

Everyone here grows basil either in their
backyards or from windowsills. In Genoa,
the streets are perfumed with the scent of
basil, nuts, and olive oil being pounded
mercilessly with a mortar and pestle into
an aromatic green sauce. It is worth it to
make the time to prepare pesto the Genovese way rather than with a modern
blender, because when fresh basil is
crushed, the scent is intoxicating. Pesto, in
fact, was taken to sea by sailors, who added
it to their bland diet of dried peas and
beans, salami, and hardened bread. That is
why today you will see pesto, made differ-
ently in each town here, folded into soups,

Two cultures—their cuisines and languages—merge at the border as Liguria gives way to the famed French Riviera, shown here at the medieval harbor town of Antibes.

salads, and entrées. I have often heard it suggested in culinary circles that Genoa makes more use of basil than any other place in the world. Whether at a farmhouse, a village townhouse, or wherever one eats in this region, trenette (ribbonlike pasta) or gnocchi with pesto or any meat or vegetable dish even flavored by a dollop of pesto is the Genovese sign of hospitality.

Olive oil is a main ingredient of pesto but it is pervasive in the Ligurian diet and it is abundant here because of inland rivers and a constant climate. Ligurian olive oil is never refined. Olives are sent to the mill and pressed the day they are gathered, instead of being stored in a warehouse for several months. In the humblest places, a plate of pasta drizzled with olive oil is considered to be a remedy for just about any ailment.

Upon their return, the sailors also hankered for fresh vegetables, which they couldn't get at sea. Ligurians, proud of their seafarers, made sure they had enough vegetables growing to satisfy these culinary yearnings. Ligurians prepared many of their vegetables by frying them. *Friggitorias* or fried-food shops could be found right at the ports. A few still exist. An old Genovese proverb, *Fritta a buona persino una scarpa,* suggests that even a shoe tastes good when it is fried.

So, a never-ending search for great flavor has always been the culinary course for the Genovese, some of the results of which you will see in this next section of *World Class Cuisine.*

La Riserva di Castel d'Appio

Trenette al Pesto alla Genovese
(Pasta with Pesto of Genoa)

Although its quaint towns border the sea, Liguria is not known for its seafood but its pesto. Here is a classic Genovese pesto sauce. At La Riserva and throughout restaurants and *trattorias* in Liguria, pesto is most often served with trenette, the local favorite ribbon pasta. The Ligurians insist that the best way to prepare the pesto is with a mortar and pestle, but a food processor will also do. What makes this recipe a bit different from most pestos in the world is that Pecorino cheese is used and potatoes and green beans are often served on the side with a dollop of pesto. In this region, pesto is not only used to dress pasta but it is incorporated in everything from morning eggs to a dish of green beans or minestrone soup.

PESTO SAUCE:

2	cloves garlic
1	cup fresh basil leaves
1	tablespoon pine nuts
	Salt and pepper
½	cup olive oil
2	ounces Pecorino cheese, cut into ½-inch cubes
½	cup grated Parmesan cheese

ASSEMBLY:

1	pound trenette or fettucine or linguini
2	medium white potatoes, peeled and sliced
½	pound green beans

- Put a large pot of salted water on the stove and bring it to a boil. When the water comes to a boil, cook the pasta, the potatoes, and the green beans together in the same pot. (If you wish, you may cook all three ingredients in separate pots to ensure that one does not cook sooner than the other.) Meanwhile, using a mortar and pestle or food processor, purée together the garlic, basil, pine nuts, and salt and pepper. Add the olive oil, and the Pecorino and Parmesan cheeses. Process until smooth to make the pesto sauce. Set aside.
- To serve, place the linguini in a serving bowl. Add the beans and potatoes and top with the pesto.

YIELD: 4 SERVINGS

It was not uncommon years ago in Italy to see a maccheronaro selling pasta from his stall set up on a street corner. Today, it is not all that different. Gourmet stores have fresh pasta now made with tomatoes or spinach and squid ink.

—Gail Greco

La Riserva di Castel d'Appio

Herbed Breast of Veal Stuffed with Mortadella and Swiss Chard

Mortadella is an Italian sausage or cold cut of the region, made with ground beef, pork, cubes of pork fat, and Italian seasonings. This meat is diced and incorporated into a breadcrumb-and-cooked-veal mixture. The mixture is then pocketed into the side of a boneless breast of veal. At La Riserva, they cook this bundle of veal in water. Veal breast meat is tough and the slow cooking in water softens its texture. However, a nice variation to cooking in water is searing the stuffed and trussed meat in a pan with a little olive oil and then roasting it in a 350° oven for about 1½ hours or until tender.

2	tablespoons olive oil
12	ounces boneless veal breast, cut into a small dice for stuffing
4	leaves Swiss chard, thinly sliced
¾	cup chopped Italian parsley
1	tablespoon chopped fresh marjoram leaves
1	large clove garlic, minced
1	small onion, finely chopped

1	cup stale Italian bread, soaked in ½ cup milk
1	cup green peas, cooked
1	cup cubed mortadella, ½-inch cubes
½	teaspoon grated nutmeg
3	eggs
½	cup pine nuts
1	cup Parmesan cheese
	Salt and pepper
1	3-pound boned veal breast, pocket cut for stuffing
	Fresh herbs and red radishes for garnish

- Heat the olive oil in a large skillet over high heat. Add the diced veal, turning to brown on all sides. Add a seasoning of salt and pepper. Add the Swiss chard, the parsley and marjoram, and the garlic and onion, stirring continuously.
- When the meat has browned, transfer the meat and the contents of the skillet to a large bowl. Add the bread with the milk, peas, mortadella, nutmeg, eggs, pine nuts, and Parmesan cheese. Season with salt and pepper and stir until well mixed.
- Stuff the mixture into the veal pocket. Fold the veal over to encase the stuffing. Tie the veal securely with kitchen string or wrap the stuffed breast in cheesecloth and tie securely. Add the stuffed veal to a large saucepan. Add enough water to cover. Turn the heat to low and simmer the stuffed veal for 1½ hours or until tender.
- When the time is up, remove the stuffed veal from the water. Cut the strings and slice the veal into ½-inch-thick pieces. Place on a serving platter and garnish with fresh herbs and red radishes.

La Riserva di Castel d'Appio

Torta di Verdure (Vegetable Pie)

FILLING:

3	tablespoons olive oil
1	clove garlic, minced
1	small onion, coarsely chopped
8	leaves Swiss chard, cut chiffonnade style
1	artichoke, top 1-inch and tough outer leaves removed and artichoke coarsely chopped
2	sprigs fennel tops, coarsely chopped
	Salt and pepper
1	cup Arborio rice
1	cup shelled peas
½	cup water
4	eggs, beaten
½	cup grated Parmesan cheese

PASTRY:

5	cups all-purpose flour
⅔	cup water
2	tablespoons olive oil
1	teaspoon salt

- Prepare the filling. Heat 1 tablespoon of the oil in a medium skillet and sauté the garlic and onions for about 2 minutes until they sweat. Add the Swiss chard, artichokes, and fennel, and season with salt and pepper. Add the rice, peas, and the water. Stir and then cover the pan and cook over medium-low heat for 15 minutes. Remove from the heat and add the eggs and Parmesan cheese. Set aside and prepare the crust.

Wine Suggestion

TORGAIO

Sangiovese Toscano

RUFFINO

BOTTLED BY
CHIANTI RUFFINO S.p.A.
PONTASSIEVE
ITALIA - 37/6FI
NET CONT. 750 ML
ALC. 12.5% BY VOL.

VINO DA TAVOLA

Torgaio Sangiovese *is an easy-to-drink, medium-bodied red wine that is delicious served slightly cool with the Torta di Verdure.*

- Preheat the oven to 350°. Place the flour on a board and make a well in the center. Pour the water, olive oil, and salt into the well. Mix the flour with your hands to incorporate. Add more water to make a soft dough. Divide the dough in half and with a rolling pin, roll out to ¼-inch thickness. Grease a 12-inch round baking pan and line it with dough. Place the filling inside. Drizzle with olive oil and roll out the second half of the dough into a round. Arrange crust over the filling. Flute the edges and bake for 25 to 30 minutes or until the crust is golden.

YIELD: 6 TO 8 SERVINGS

La Riserva di Castel d'Appio

Orange Chestnut Cake with Apples and Pine Nuts

Chestnut flour may be found at some specialty food stores, through mail order houses, or in Italian delicatessans. Avoid stale flour as the chestnut flavor becomes bitter.

2	tablespoons olive oil, plus ¼ cup
2	cups chestnut flour
4	cups water
	Salt
1	Golden Delicious apple, cored and cut into thin slices
1	tablespoon orange zest
½	cup pine nuts
½	cup raisins
	Fresh strawberries and mint leaves for garnish

- In a large bowl, combine the chestnut flour and water with a dash of salt. Whisk the mixture until incorporated. Allow it to stand for 2 hours at room temperature.
- Preheat the oven to 375°. Grease an 11x13x½-inch baking pan with the 2 tablespoons olive oil.
- Pour in the chestnut flour mixture and top with the sliced apples, orange zest, pine nuts, and raisins. Pour the remaining olive oil over the top.
- Bake for 1 hour. Slice and garnish each serving with strawberries and mint leaves.

YIELD: 6 TO 8 SERVINGS

La Riserva di Castel d'Appio

Apricot Jellyroll Cake

Any fruit preserves will do nicely for this cake. Jellyroll desserts are easy to do and always look professional but inviting.

4	eggs
1	cup sugar, plus more for sprinkling
2	cups all-purpose flour
1	teaspoon baking powder
1	teaspoon lemon zest
1½	cups apricot preserves
	Confectioners' sugar
	Fresh strawberries and mint leaves for garnish

- Preheat the oven to 375°. In a large bowl, beat the eggs with the sugar until they are pale. Gradually whisk in the flour, then baking powder, and finally the lemon zest.
- Line a standard jellyroll pan with parchment paper and grease well. Pour the cake batter into the pan and bake for 15 minutes or until a tester inserted comes clean.
- Dampen a tea towel with cool water and sprinkle sugar over the towel. Unmold the cake onto the towel. Spread the cake with apricot or other preserves. Use the towel as a pusher to roll up the cake onto itself. Press gently to hold the roll together. Carefully remove the towel. Dust the top of the cake with confectioners' sugar and decorate the top with strawberries.
- To serve, slice the cake on the diagonal into ½-inch-thick pieces. Garnish with more strawberries and fresh mint.

YIELD: 8 TO 10 SERVINGS

Chez Greco

Ravioli Dolci

Made with a sweet dough, the ravioli are stuffed with citrus flavorings and chocolate, and the very Ligurian touch of pine nuts. You may serve this with a dollop of whipped cream or crème fraîche, or a chocolate sauce. Since Ligurians love to stuff an uncountable mixture of ingredients into ravioli and other pastas and meats, I thought this recipe from my own family files fit well in this section of *World Class Cuisine.*

DOUGH:

4	eggs
¾	cup sugar
2-2⅔	cups all-purpose flour
1	teaspoon baking powder
½	cup (1 stick) butter, cut into pats
	Grated peel of ½ lemon
	Grated peel of ½ orange

FILLING:

12	ounces Ricotta cheese
⅓	cup sugar
3	ounces semisweet chocolate, finely grated
¼	cup candied lemon or orange peel, finely chopped
2	tablespoons pine nuts
1	tablespoon Grand Marnier

ASSEMBLY:

	Confectioners' sugar
	Whipped cream or chocolate sauce for garnish

Wine Suggestion

The classic orange flavors combined with the richness and depth of fine Cognac, allow **Grand Marnier** *to blend perfectly with the sweetness of the Ravioli Dolci.*

- Make the dough. In a large mixing bowl, beat together the eggs and sugar. When smooth, add the flour, baking powder, butter, and citrus peels and mix well to incorporate. Allow the dough to rest in a cool place for about 30 minutes. Meanwhile prepare the filling.
- In a large bowl, beat together the Ricotta and the sugar until smooth. Add the rest of the ingredients except the confectioners' sugar and garnishes. Set aside and create the ravioli.
- Preheat the oven to 350°. Divide the dough in half and roll out each piece into a ¼-inch-thick sheet. Place rounded teaspoonfuls of the filling onto 1 of the sheets, about 2 inches apart. When all of the filling is used up, cover with the second pasta sheet. Press this sheet down with your fingers, all around the mounds. Using a pastry wheel cutter, cut a square around each mound to form a 3x3-inch ravioli.
- Place the ravioli on a greased baking sheet and bake for 20 minutes or until golden brown. Remove the tray from the oven and allow the ravioli to cool on the sheet over wire racks. Dust generously with confectioners' sugar and serve.

YIELD: 8 SERVINGS, 16 RAVIOLI

LAZIO

——— ❦ ❦ ❦ ———

Simple Fare Contrasts This Triumphant Region

*T*he extravagant Trevi Fountain, the posh Piazza Navona, the stylish Spanish Steps, the colossal Coliseum. Rome is the largest city by far in this region, with 80 percent of Lazio residents living there. It seems odd that with all this grandeur, the food of its people always has been and still is today more plain and simple—more peasant than gourmet—based on pasta, dried beans, and meats.

But the people of Lazio put more of an emphasis on conviviality rather than on sophisticated food preparations. Lazians go out to restaurants in droves to enjoy themselves, and to express themselves, and to eat well. All year long there are feasts in the region, from the polenta festival to the seafood festival, where tons of fish are fried in a single gigantic pan. The food here is cooked without frills, only celebration, despite the region's rich resources.

Just south of Tuscany, Lazio has hills for olive growing; flatlands for producing vegetables; mountains for chestnuts and mushrooms; lakes, rivers, and the sea for fish; and unlike Liguria, lots of pastures for livestock and rich volcanic soil for grape

growing. Rome has many ornamental and fruit trees in its more tropical climate.

Sheep and pork are popular meats, and Romans make good use even of the animals' organs. Liver, for example, is grilled and served with a squeeze of citrus juice or sautéed with onions and glazed with wine. Lamb is the main meat here and a famous dish is *abbacchio,* very young milk-fed lamb roasted or grilled and eaten with the fingers. *Porchetta,* or suckling pig, is also very popular, flavored with rosemary, anise seed, and garlic. *Porchetta* was traditionally spit-roasted over a wood fire and eaten during religious festivals.

Spaghetti reigns as the pasta of choice with two preparations that are particularly of Lazian character. Spaghetti carbonara is made with bacon, oil, eggs, peppers, and Pecorino cheese. It is reputed to have been a dish made by the *Carbonari* or coal men of the Lazio forest. Probably the most famous dish of the region is spaghetti *all'amatriciana.* The sauce is made from bacon, onions, tomatoes, chili, and Pecorino cheese. A bowl of Lazio's renowned *stracciatella* (a consommé with beaten eggs), a salad, and the

The Spanish Steps in Rome come alive with azaleas each spring.

spaghetti carbonara make for a complete meal.

Artichokes are one of the most sought-after vegetables of the area, usually stuffed with mint, oil, and white wine. Young broad beans or fava beans are usually eaten raw with grated cheese. And the Lazians enjoy snacking on *supplì* or balls of rice and Mozzarella rolled in breadcrumbs and deep-fried. Garlic is a mainstay and popular with spaghetti and olive oil. Even dessert is of a common-sense nature. People buy fresh Ricotta cheese in little baskets direct from the shepherds and mix it with sugar and brewed coffee or with honey and cinnamon.

To give you a taste of Lazio, the recipes here are a mixture of simple ingredients with a gourmet flair.

Le Grand Hôtel

Artichokes Roman Style

8	artichokes
1	cup lemon juice
	Salt
2	tablespoons mint, chopped
1	cup chopped parsley
½	cup extra virgin olive oil
3	cloves garlic
1	cup white wine
1	cup chicken broth

- Clean the artichokes. Remove the coarse outer leaves. Clean the stems, shaving them with a potato peeler to expose the tender interior. Using a sharp knife, make an even cut across the top of the artichoke, cutting off the top parts of the leaves.
- Rub the artichokes with lemon juice and place them in a bowl, with just enough water to cover. Add the remaining lemon juice.
- Let the artichokes sit in the lemon and water mixture for about 30 minutes. Remove them from the liquid and pat the artichokes dry with a tea towel.
- When the artichokes are dried, open them up like a flower, and season with salt, mint, and parsley.
- Cook the artichokes in a large saucepan with the olive oil and garlic. Cook over medium heat.

When the garlic turns golden brown, add the wine and allow the liquid to simmer until the wine has evaporated, about 5 to 6 minutes.

- Add the broth to the saucepan and cover the pan. Simmer over low heat for about 40 minutes.

YIELD: 4 SERVINGS

Hôtel Lord Byron

Shrimp-and-Sole Florentine Rolls with Seafood Zabaglione

One of Italy's greatest gifts to the world is the foamy custard called zabaglione. The French profusely adopted the use of the custard in many of their dishes. In France, it is commonly known as sabayon.

SEAFOOD ZABAGLIONE:

3	egg yolks
½	cup fish stock
¼	cup white wine

ROLLS:

1	tablespoon extra virgin olive oil
½	pound fresh spinach
	Salt and pepper
8	filets of fresh sole, pounded with a mallet
20	medium shrimp, peeled and deveined
1	cup white wine
3	cups fish stock

ASSEMBLY:

¾	cup whipped cream

Wine Suggestion

LIBAIO

da uve Chardonnay e Pinot Grigio di Toscana

RUFFINO

Libaio, an all-purpose, dry white blend of Chardonnay and Pinot Grigio, is rich in character and well balanced for the shrimp and sole.

- Make the zabaglione. In a medium saucepan, whisk together the 3 egg yolks and the ½ cup of fish stock. Whisk in the white wine and cook over medium heat until thickened. Set aside.
- In a medium skillet, heat the olive oil and add the spinach, cooking quickly, just until it softens and wilts. Season with salt and pepper. Remove from the heat and set aside.
- Cut the sole filets into ½-inch wide strips, ending up with 16 strips. Pound to flatten. Wrap each shrimp with a strip, reserving 4 shrimps without a wrapping for use later.
- Poach the rolls in the fish stock over medium-high heat for 1 to 2 minutes or until they are firm.
- Lay the spinach into individual heat-proof serving plates. Place four rolls on top of each dish. Fold the whipped cream into the zabaglione, adding about 2 tablespoons of the zabagalione mixture to each dish. Pass quickly under a broiler, just to turn golden, and serve. Top each with a reserved shrimp.

Hôtel Lord Byron

Baked Capon-and-Truffle Bread Soup with Lentils

The Relais le Jardin restaurant at the splendid Hôtel Lord Byron blends the sophistication of metropolitan Rome with ancient international traditions, and this example of using one of the oldest forms of pulse—lentils—with the truffle paste, is a good example of the old with the new. Basically, you are making a chicken soup with lentils and mushrooms, covering it with a simple dough crust, and baking it. This is a most Roman way of eating soup.

Wine Suggestion

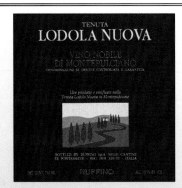
CHICKEN BROTH:

1	whole capon or chicken (about 3½ pounds)
	Water to cover
1	large carrot, coarsely chopped
1	rib celery, coarsely chopped
2	cloves garlic, coarsely chopped
2	whole medium tomatoes, seeds removed, coarsely chopped
1	ounce dried porcini mushrooms
1	cup white wine
2	sprigs each: rosemary, parsley, sage, and basil
1	tablespoon black peppercorns
½	teaspoon cinnamon
2	whole cloves

LENTILS:

1	cup lentils, rinsed and picked over
2	tablespoons extra virgin olive oil
2	tablespoons chopped prosciutto
1	sage leaf
1	clove garlic, minced
1	shallot, minced
½	cup white wine
2	teaspoons truffle paste
½	cup shredded radicchio
1	cup assorted wild mushrooms, chopped and sautéed in butter
	Salt and white pepper

CRUST:

1½	pounds all-purpose flour
1	ounce yeast
2	tablespoons olive oil
	Warm water
	Salt
	Egg wash

- Prepare the capon broth by placing the chicken into a large stockpot and covering with water. Add the carrot, celery, garlic, tomatoes, mushrooms, white wine, herbs, peppercorns, cinna-

The fettucine with zucchini blossoms

mon, and cloves, and poach the ingredients over medium-high heat until the chicken is tender and cooked through, about 30 minutes. Remove the capon from the pot and cut the chicken into pieces, pulling the meat from the bones. Discard the bones and cut the chicken up into bite-size pieces or fine strips. Strain the broth and reserve. Discard the vegetables.

- In a medium saucepan, cook the lentils in the chicken broth for about 40 minutes or until tender. Set aside.
- In a large skillet, heat the olive oil and add the prosciutto, sage, garlic, and the shallot. Cook for 2 minutes and add the white wine and the cooked lentils with their broth. Add the truffle paste, the radicchio, the mushrooms, and the chicken. Season with salt and pepper.
- Preheat the oven to 425°. Meanwhile, make the soup crust. Combine the flour, yeast, and olive oil, adding enough water slowly to make a smooth dough. Add salt to taste. Form into a ball and roll out the dough to ¼-inch thickness. Brush the egg wash around the rim of 8 individual soup bowls. Ladle the capon soup into the bowls. Arrange a piece of pastry crust atop each bowl, covering the bowl entirely. Brush with more egg wash. Bake for 5 minutes or until the crust puffs and turns a golden brown.

YIELD: 8 SERVINGS

Fettucine with Zucchini Blossoms Julienne and Eggplant Sauce

2	tablespoons olive oil
½	shallot, minced
8	zucchini blossoms, cut julienne
1	small eggplant, peeled, sliced, salted, and allowed to sit 30 minutes, then rinsed and cut into bite-size pieces
2	tablespoons chopped basil
½	cup white wine
1	finely chopped chili pepper
1	medium peeled ripe tomato, cut into bite-size pieces
	Salt and pepper
12	ounces fresh fettucine noodles
¼	cup grated Parmesan cheese
1	tablespoon heavy cream
1	tablespoon butter, melted
⅛	teaspoon saffron threads
	Fresh basil leaves for garnish

- In a large skillet, heat the olive oil and sauté the shallot until translucent. Add the strips of zucchini blossom, the eggplant, and the basil. Pour in the white wine. Cook the mixture for about 10 minutes over medium heat and add the chili pepper and tomato. Season with salt and pepper.
- In a large pot of boiling salted water, cook the fettucine. Drain and place the pasta in the pan with the eggplant sauce. Add the grated cheese, the cream, and the butter. Mix in the saffron. Place the pasta in serving plates and garnish with a basil leaf.

YIELD: 4 SERVINGS

Le Grand Hôtel

Bucatini all'Amatriciana (Spaghetti in a Spicy Tomato-and-Bacon Sauce)

This dish hails from an area called Abruzzi near Amatrice in Lazio and is significant for its unusual assortment of flavors from bacon to hot pepper. Bucatini is the name of a spaghetti that is thicker than most and has a hole through the length of each strand, similar to perciatelli. Bucatini's long, hollow style is widely available in the United States and is chosen in a recipe because the sauce can actually get between the pasta and into the hollow, instead of just sitting on top.

¼	cup olive oil
2	cloves garlic, lightly crushed
¼	cup sliced onion
1	small, dried, crushed, hot chili pepper
8	ounces bacon strips
½	cup white wine
1½	pound tomatoes, peeled
1	pound bucatini pasta or perciatelli
¼	cup grated Pecorino cheese
¼	cup Parmesan cheese

Wine Suggestion

The wonderful berry flavors of the **Simi Rosé of Cabernet Sauvignon** *marry well with the tastes found in this classic pasta dish— bucatini.*

- Heat the olive oil in a shallow saucepan and sauté the garlic and onion. Add the chili pepper and cook until browned. Add the bacon and cook until the bacon browns over medium-high heat. Pour the wine into the pan and cook until it evaporates. Add the tomatoes and cook the entire mixture on medium heat for about 10 minutes.
- Cook the bucatini in boiling salted water until *al dente.* Drain and serve with the bacon and tomato sauce. Sprinkle with the Pecorino and Parmesan cheeses and serve.

YIELD: 4 SERVINGS

The bucatini pasta, Veal Chops Stuffed with Taleggio Cheese and Warm Romaine Lettuce (see recipe on page 27), and Artichokes Roman Style (see recipe on page 20)

Hôtel Lord Byron

Roasted Lamb Chops with Artichoke Purée and Mint Sauce

Artichokes have been a Roman tradition for centuries. It seems that you can find artichokes, or *carciofi* as the Romans call them, in every Roman snack bar. This is a splendid dish, with such a flourish of mint that the best way to describe it is refreshing.

*W*ine Suggestion

TENUTA
SANTEDAME

CHIANTI CLASSICO
DENOMINAZIONE DI ORIGINE CONTROLLATA E GARANTITA

BOTTLED BY CHIANTI RUFFINO
SpA - PONTASSIEVE - ITALIA - 326/FI
PRODUCT OF ITALY

750 ml ℮   **TENIMENTI**
RUFFINO   ALC. 12.5% BY VOL.

Santedame is a Chianti Classico with the depth and intensity of flavor that makes it an excellent match for the roasted lamb.

ARTICHOKE PURÉE:

2	teaspoons extra virgin olive oil
1	clove garlic
½	shallot, minced
4	artichokes, peeled, cleaned, poached in boiling water until tender, and sliced apart
¼	cup white wine
¼	cup demi-glace (or see recipe for Quick Brown Sauce, page 185)
2	skinned, boiled white potatoes, peeled and quartered
	Salt and pepper

LAMB:

1	tablespoon extra virgin olive oil
2	pounds loin of lamb
1	large carrot, sliced julienne
1	rib celery, sliced julienne
1	leek, white part only
1	shallot
1	clove garlic
½	teaspoon fresh rosemary
½	teaspoon fresh thyme
¼	cup plus 2 tablespoons finely chopped fresh mint, and mint leaves for garnish
¾	cup white wine

- Begin the recipe by making the artichoke purée. In a medium skillet over medium-high heat, heat the olive oil and sauté the garlic and shallot until translucent. Add the sliced artichokes and stew in the pan for about 2 minutes or until lightly browned. Douse the pan with the wine and then the demi-glace broth. Cook the mixture over medium-high heat until the artichokes are very soft and brown. When cooked, toss the potatoes in with the artichokes. Season all with salt and pepper. Set the artichokes aside and keep the mixture warm until serving time.

- Prepare the lamb. Heat the 1 tablespoon of olive oil in a large saucepan. Sauté the lamb until browned on all sides. Preheat the oven to 400°.
- Place the carrot, celery, leek, and shallot in the bottom of a large baking dish to form a bed for the loin. Add the garlic, rosemary, thyme, and the ¼ cup of chopped mint. Season overall with salt and pepper. Bake for about 10 minutes, basting with the white wine. When the lamb has cooked (should be rare inside) remove it from the oven and set aside, keeping it warm. Collect the juices from the pan and remove the fat.
- Slice the loin into ½-inch thick chops. Place the artichoke purée evenly among the 4 individual serving plates. Add a chop or 2 to each plate and garnish with more fresh mint.

YIELD: 4 SERVINGS

Le Grand Hôtel

Veal Chops Stuffed with Taleggio Cheese and Warm Romaine Lettuce

Taleggio is a semisoft cheese with a pungent taste. It is recommended for use with salad greens, hence it goes very well with the endive. Since Roman endive is unavailable, substitute with romaine lettuce or curly spinach, which is much more similar than Belgian endive. Taleggio is a more readily available Italian ingredient but you may use any soft cheese that has an intense, sharp flavor.

½	cup olive oil, divided
8	ounces romaine lettuce, coarsely chopped
2	pounds thick veal chops (1 per person)
1½	cups Taleggio cheese, cut into ¼-inch-thick pieces
	Salt and pepper
	All-purpose flour
½	cup white wine
2	tablespoons demi-glace

- Preheat the oven to 325°. Heat ¼ cup of the olive oil in a medium skillet over high heat. When the oil is hot, sauté the romaine lettuce in the pan, just until it wilts. (It should retain its color and only change its texture.) When the leaves wilt, turn the heat down to a simmer, just to keep the lettuce warm.
- Cut pockets in the veal for stuffing. Drain the lettuce from the pan and stuff the chops evenly with lettuce and cheese until all are used up. Season the chops with salt and pepper and coat lightly with flour to keep from sticking.
- Add the remaining olive oil to the same skillet and heat over a high flame. Sear the chops on both sides, until browned, about 1 to 2 minutes per side. Deglaze the pan with the wine and demi-glace (or use Quick Brown Sauce, see page 185).
- Place the chops in the oven (in the skillet or in a clean baking dish) and cook for 5 to 6 minutes or more for desired doneness. (The veal needs only to warm through and the cheese to melt, but the meat may be as rare or cooked as desired.)
- When the meat is tender, and the sauce nicely thickened, serve the chops with your favorite side dishes.

YIELD: 4 SERVINGS

The roasted lamb chops (see recipe on page 26) against the backdrop of a verdant mural scene in Le Jardin restaurant at Hôtel Lord Byron in Rome

Almond-Tulips-with-Blossoms-of-Citrus Mousse

The combination of delicious citrus with the warm toffee or caramel biscuit offers a delicate dessert fit for a Roman god and certainly suitable to your Roman meal at home. Actually, you're making a thin, lacy cookie, shaped similarly to an almond tuille, but as you cool the warmed toffee over a cup, ruffle it up a bit to give that tulip appearance, then add a "blossom" (scoop) of citrus mousse and serve with your favorite caramel sauce.

MOUSSE:

2	egg yolks
¾	cup sugar
½	cup orange juice
2	tablespoons white wine
	Grated peel of 1 orange
1	tablespoon powdered gelatin or 1 leaf gelatin, softened in cool water
¼	cup heavy cream, whipped
2	egg whites and 2 teaspoons lemon juice, whipped to soft peaks

TULIP:

⅓	cup water
½	cup firmly packed brown sugar
½	cup confectioners' sugar
½	cup almond paste
1	tablespoon hazelnuts, finely chopped
¾	cup all-purpose flour
¼	cup melted butter

ASSEMBLY:

| Chopped hazelnuts for garnish |
| Caramel, strawberry, or raspberry sauce |
| Fresh fruit for garnish |

🌿 🌿 🌿

- Make the mousse. Heat the egg yolks in a double boiler, whipping them together constantly with the sugar, orange juice, and white wine until thickened and light in color, about 10 minutes. Remove from the heat. Continue whipping the mixture until it becomes thick and creamy. Mix in the orange peel, gelatin, whipped cream, and whipped egg whites. Place the mixture in the refrigerator uncovered until it is chilled, about 1 hour.

- In a small saucepan prepare the tulip by making a syrup. Heat together the water and brown sugar over medium-high heat until well combined and syrupy. Remove from the heat and allow the mixture to cool. Stir in the confectioners' sugar, the almond paste, hazelnuts, and the flour, until well mixed. Add the butter and pour into a glass bowl to cool for 2 hours in the refrigerator.

- Preheat the oven to 400°. Grease and line with parchment paper a 9x13-inch baking pan and spread very thin tablespoonfuls of the syrup onto the pan, 1 inch apart. Bake for 10 minutes or until the syrup has browned and is still pliable. While still warm, turn each piece of the cooked toffee over a cup and ruffle up the edges. You will get about 4 large cookies.

- Line a dinner plate with a drizzle of caramel or strawberry or raspberry sauce. Using an ice cream scoop, fill each tulip with the citrus mousse. Sprinkle with nuts for garnish and any variety of fresh fruit.

YIELD: 4 SERVINGS

If you like, you can add a caramel cage to the top of this dessert by crisscrossing hot caramel sauce in thin lines over the bottom of a soup ladle. Let the caramel harden and then remove from ladle.

Hôtel Lord Byron

Panettone-and-Prunes Brandied Soufflé with Hazelnut Sauce

Originating in Milan, *panettone* is a ubiquitous yeast bread served throughout Italy, especially during Christmas time. Bursting with the flavors of sweet citron, pine nuts, and anise, it is the highlight of breakfasts served whenever my family gets together. I have even made French toast with *panettone*. The Armagnac adds a hint of French to this delicate dessert. The prunes need to soak in the brandy for 30 minutes before preparing the sauce and the soufflé. Serve the soufflé with your favorite sweet sauce. Chef Antonio Sciullo recommends chocolate, toffee, or caramel sauces as a substitute for his hazelnut sauce.

There is a love story behind the origins of *panettone.* The only dowry a poor baker could provide his daughter was his skills as a cook. When his daughter wished to marry a distinguished nobleman, the baker—whose name was Tonio—provided all of the materials to make a sweet yeast bread or *pane. Pane de Tonio*—or Tonio's bread—emerged over the years as *panettone.* Tonio made a fortune with his bread and his daughter found a perfect match.

PRUNES:

| ⅔ | cup pitted prunes, cut into bite-size pieces |
| 1 | cup Armagnac brandy |

HAZELNUT SAUCE:

2	ounces cocoa butter
½	cup toasted hazelnuts, ground to a powder
¾	cup sweetened cocoa powder
½	cup confectioners' sugar

SOUFFLÉ:

½	cup pastry cream (see recipe page 186)
3	egg yolks
1	teaspoon vanilla extract
1¼	cups toasted panettone, cut into ½-inch dice
8	egg whites
¾	cup confectioners' sugar, plus more for coating
	Granulated sugar for coating

- Soak the prunes in the brandy for at least 30 minutes, then drain. Make the hazelnut sauce. In a medium saucepan, mix all of the ingredients for the sauce, melting and incorporating them over medium-high heat. Set aside and prepare the soufflé.
- Mix the pastry cream with the egg yolks and vanilla. Fold in the soaked prunes and the panettone. Stir well.
- Preheat the oven to 400°. In another bowl, whip the egg whites with the confectioners' sugar just until incorporated. Gently fold in the cream-and-panettone mixture.
- Grease 8 (10-ounce) custard cups and coat with granulated sugar. Fill each cup three-quarters full with the soufflé mixture. Place the cups in the oven on a baking sheet and bake for 20 to 30 minutes or until browned and puffed to nearly double. Sprinkle with confectioners' sugar. Warm the hazelnut sauce or a sauce of your choice and serve.

YIELD: 8 SERVINGS

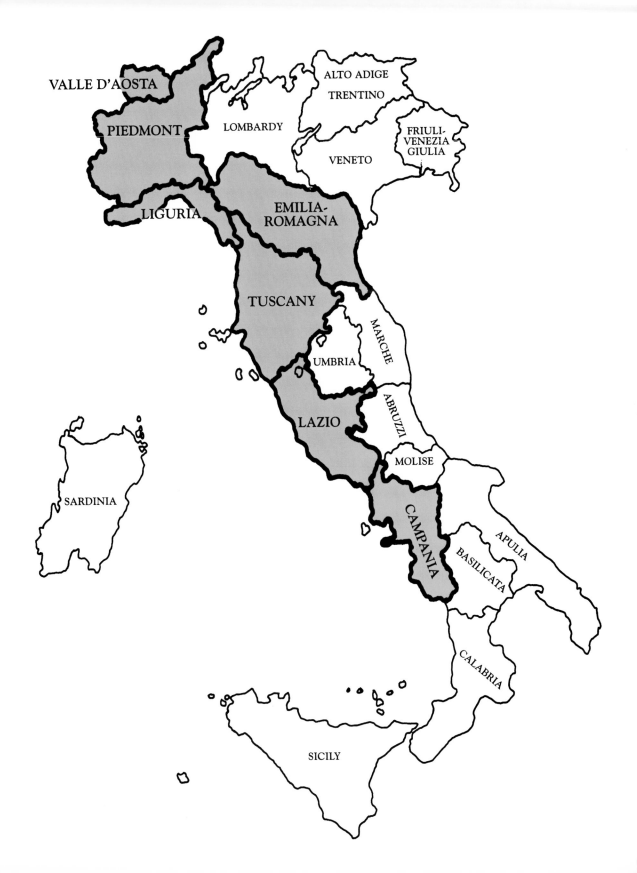

VALLE D'AOSTA

PIEDMONT

LOMBARDY

ALTO ADIGE

TRENTINO

FRIULI-
VENEZIA
GIULIA

VENETO

LIGURIA

EMILIA-
ROMAGNA

TUSCANY

MARCHE

UMBRIA

LAZIO

ABRUZZI

MOLISE

CAMPANIA

APULIA

BASILICATA

SARDINIA

CALABRIA

SICILY

CAMPANIA

Pizza, Pasta, Pomodoro, and the Smile of the Moon

Vesuvius, a rumbling volcano that erupted centuries ago, leaving behind rich black soil, is probably largely responsible for the cuisine of Campania, which has certainly had a major effect on what the entire world eats. Tomatoes grow everywhere in this region, having arrived in the sixteenth century. Today, Campania's tomatoes or *pomodori* are exported all over the world. But in Campania they are almost always used fresh. Even in winter, you can find tomato sauce made with tomatoes dried in the sun on kitchen balconies all over the province. Tomatoes are the basis of Campanian cuisine, prepared with a variety of other ingredients. Some two hundred years after their arrival here, these ripe red jewels were paired with bread and the world was introduced to a thing called pizza, an invention from Naples, the heart of Campania.

Pizzerias in Naples are places of pride where proprietors still often sing their way through the stretching and shaping of the dough as it spirals through the air at the twist of the chef's wrist. Pizza is served mainly in its simplest version—alla

Positano beach scene

margherita. It was, in fact, a royal dish, favored by kings and queens visiting Naples from France and Spain.

Campania includes the beautiful blue Amalfi coast that stretches from Lazio and opens to southern Italy. The dry climate produces quality grain, and so it was a natural industry for Naples to make pasta at its many factories that are still in business today. Pasta—or macaroni as it has been traditionally called—is often eaten twice a day—in different forms. Naples gave us the cooking method *al dente* or cooking the pasta "to the tooth"—chewy, not soft. Unlike Liguria, where pasta is topped with pesto, and Lazio, where olive oil is drizzled on top, in Campania, tomato sauce is the choice for pasta. Sauces are often combined with vegetables and paired with pasta shapes depending on the texture of the sauce. A thicker, sometimes meat-filled sauce called ragu—that cooks for a long time—is often poured over pasta.

Cheese is another of Campania's main products. Sheep, cows, goats, and buffalo provide the resources for a variety of cheeses including Provolone and particularly fresh Mozzarella. Mozzarella di bufala, or fresh Mozzarella made from buffalo's milk, comes in small bundles packed in water.

Meat is not as popular in this region as in others, but when it is served, it is often made *alla pizzaiola*, cooked in tomatoes and fresh garlic. Seafood is paired with pasta such as spaghetti *alle vongole* (with clam sauce). Another popular dish is fried calamari.

In southern Italy, the people have been categorized as warm, passionate, generous, superstitious, and wrapped up in the family. They believe that the quality of their soil, their air, and the moon that smiles over their grazing herds contribute to the superiority of their harvests and products. And as you work with the recipes on the next few pages from chefs in this region, I think you will see that what they do with those foods allows all of us to grin back up at the heavens.

Augustus Caesar surveys the idyllic Isle of Capri, along the Amalfi coast of Campania.

The Belvedere Caruso

Baked-Cheese-and-Genoa-Salami Roll

Although this is served at the restaurant as an appetizer, you can also jazz up a brunch with this pancakelike dish. Filled with salami, it contains Mozzarella and Ricotta cheeses and is baked up jellyroll style.

FILLING:

2	tablespoons butter
3	tablespoons all-purpose flour
1	cup scalded milk
¼	cup Genoa or other salami
¼	cup Ricotta cheese
¼	cup shredded Mozzarella
1	tablespoon grated Parmesan cheese
	Salt and pepper
1	egg white

PANCAKE:

4	eggs
2	tablespoons water
½	teaspoon salt
2	tablespoons butter

ASSEMBLY:

	Egg wash
	Parsley for garnish

🌿 🌿 🌿

- In a small saucepan, melt the butter over low heat and add the flour, making a roux. Stir the mixture until frothy. Remove from the heat and add the scalded milk. Return the pan to the heat and cook the mixture, stirring vigorously with a wire whisk, until it is smooth. Simmer the sauce (over low heat) for 5 minutes.
- Stir in the salami and Ricotta and Mozzarella cheeses. Add the Parmesan cheese and season with salt and pepper. Cover and place in the refrigerator to chill while preparing the pancake.
- In a medium bowl, beat the eggs with the water and salt, until the mixture foams. Place a non-stick 10-inch crêpe pan over medium heat until the pan is hot. Add the butter and swirl it around the pan, making sure to cover the bottom and a little of the sides well. Pour in the egg mixture and cook, lifting the cooked portion from the edge of the pan, allowing the liquid egg to run under and onto the hot pan. When the pancake is set, slide it over and cook the other side. Remove the pancake from the pan.
- Spread the pancake evenly with the cheese filling, leaving a 1-inch border free of the spread. Roll the pancake up jellyroll style and chill in the refrigerator for 30 minutes to set.
- When the time is up, preheat the oven to 375°. Grease a 9x13-inch glass baking dish and cut the pancake into 6 even slices. Arrange them flat-side up on the dish. Brush the tops of each piece with egg wash and sprinkle generously with Parmesan cheese. Bake for 15 minutes or until lightly browned. Garnish with parsley and serve immediately.

YIELD: 6 SERVINGS

Pulling in the catch of the day from the rich waters off the Amalfi coast

Southern Italian food was considered poor and unhealthy (social workers were sent to encourage Italian-Americans to change their eating habits) until American dieticians discovered the merits of a healthy, low-cholesterol Mediterranean diet. Now it is one of the most fashionable cuisines.

—Claudia Roden, *The Good Food of Italy*

Grand Hôtel Cocumella

Scampi-and-Orange Salad

Light and good-looking, this simple salad makes a great appetizer or luncheon plate.

12	extra-large shrimp
2	large oranges
2	tablespoons extra virgin olive oil
	Juice of ½ to 1 orange
	Salt
	Minced parsley for garnish
	Orange sections for garnish

- Boil or steam the shrimp with their shells on just until they turn pink. Remove the shells. Chop the shrimp into bite-size pieces. Set aside.

- Peel the oranges, separate into sections, and dice. In a bowl, toss the oranges and shrimp together. Add the olive oil. Add the orange juice and salt to taste. Garnish with the parsley and a few orange sections.

YIELD: 4 SERVINGS

A view of the Amalfi coast from Villa Rufolo in the tiny mountaintop town of Ravello, home also to the Belvedere Caruso's comfortable restaurant and hotel

Le Sirenuse

Eggplant-and-Mozzarella Roulades

When looking for an easy, tasty appetizer—the kind that you cannot stop eating like potato chips—this is it.

1	medium eggplant
½	cup all-purpose flour
1	cup sunflower oil
6	ounces Mozzarella cheese, cut into ¼-inch slices
1	medium bunch basil leaves

- Slice the eggplant into thin (¼-inch or so) slices. Soak slices in salted water for 15 minutes. Drain and dry the eggplant slices with a paper towel.
- Preheat the oven to 350°. Coat the eggplant with flour. In a medium skillet, heat the sunflower oil and fry the eggplant slices until golden brown. Drain the eggplant on paper towels. (Note that coating the eggplant with flour keeps the vegetable from absorbing so much oil.)
- Roll each slice up with a slice of Mozzarrella and a basil leaf. Place the roulades in a greased baking dish and cook for 10 minutes or until cheese just starts to melt. Serve immediately.

YIELD: 4 TO 6 APPETIZER SERVINGS

The village of Monte Pertuso, high in the mountains above Positano

- Cut the eggplant into ¼- to ½-inch diagonal slices. Soak them in salted water for about 15 minutes. Drain and dry on a paper towel. Heat the sunflower oil in a large skillet and sauté the eggplant slices until browned on both sides. Drain well on a paper towel.
- Preheat the oven to 350°. Spoon a layer of tomato sauce into a 9x13-inch ovenproof glass baking dish (or any size or shape you desire; I have even made this in a ceramic quiche dish.) Follow with layers of eggplant, Mozzarella, fresh basil, and Parmesan cheese. Repeat layers, ending with tomato sauce on top and another sprinkling of basil and cheese. Bake for 15 minutes or until the cheese is fully melted and turning brown.

YIELD: 6 TO 8 SERVINGS

Le Sirenuse

Parmigiana di Melanzane (Baked Eggplant with Tomato Sauce)

I have made baked eggplant parmigiana for many years, switching over from the fried version to simply cooking the eggplant first in the oven with a sprinkling of olive oil. This recipe from Le Sirenuse is the classic way to make this dish.

2	pounds eggplant
2¼	cups sunflower oil
2	cups homemade Italian tomato sauce
2	cups diced Mozzarella cheese
1	small bunch fresh basil
1	cup grated Parmesan cheese

Grand Hôtel Cocumella

Swordfish-and-Eggplant Rolls Mozzarella

The swordfish and Mozzarella cheese make this appetizer a comfortable and gentle one to serve before a meal with heavier, richer foods.

BREADCRUMB FILLING:

1¼	cups plain breadcrumbs
¼	cup olive oil
2	cloves garlic, minced
2	tablespoons minced parsley
1	teaspoon salt
	Juice of 2 lemons

Card players at the Sedil Dominova club in Sorrento, home also to the Grand Hotel Cocumella

ASSEMBLY:

4	petite eggplants
1	cup vegetable or sunflower oil or more for frying
1	pound swordfish, cut into ⅛- to ¼-inch slices
8	ounces fresh Mozzarella
2	tablespoons minced fresh basil for garnish
1	medium tomato for garnish

🌿 🌿 🌿

- In a small bowl, mix together the breadcrumbs, oil, garlic, parsley, salt, and the lemon juice until the mixture is well combined. It should be slightly moist. (Add a little more oil if necessary.)
- Slice the eggplants lengthwise into ¼-inch-thick or up to ½-inch-thick slices, thin enough to roll. Heat the vegetable oil in a frying pan and sauté the eggplant until golden brown, turning to cook both sides. Drain well on paper towels.
- Preheat the oven to 350°. Place the eggplant slices on the work surface. Place a slice of swordfish on each piece, followed by a slice of Mozzarella. Add 1 or 2 teaspoons of the bread-crumb mixture, spreading it over the surface. Roll the slices and place in an ovenproof glass baking dish, tucking the fastened side face down. Bake for 10 minutes or until the seafood

is cooked and the cheese is melted. Serve immediately, garnished with fresh basil and a wedge of tomato.

───────

YIELD: 4 TO 6 SERVINGS

*W*ine *Suggestion*

Swordfish requires a wine with the depth and complexity of Cabreo La Pietra from the Tuscan Estates of Ruffino.

Arsenale Restaurant

Pizza Margherita with Arugula and Smoked Salmon

The Campania region is home to pizza and here the Arsenale Restaurant offers a version of the traditional tomato sauce and Mozzarella pie with a few interesting toppings. They bake their pizza in a wood-burning oven at Arsenale, but just be sure your oven is very hot. If you prefer not to bother with making the dough yourself, buy pizza dough prepackaged in the supermarket or specialty food store.

Pizza in the kitchen at the Arsenale Restaurant in Minori

DOUGH:

1	package active dry yeast
1	cup warm water
4	cups all-purpose flour, divided in half
½	teaspoon salt

TOPPING:

½	pound Mozzarella cheese, fresh preferred
2	medium ripe red tomatoes, seeds removed, diced
3	ounces smoked salmon, cut into thin slices
2	tablespoons olive oil
1	cup coarsely chopped arugula

- Dissolve the yeast in the water. Slowly add half the flour or more, adding enough to form a soft, smooth, and elastic dough. (Add more flour if the dough is too sticky.) Grease a bowl and add the dough to the bowl. Cover with a cloth and leave in a warm place to rise for about 30 minutes. Sift the remaining flour and salt together and make a pit in the middle of this mixture.

- When the dough has risen, place it in the middle of the flour and mix. Knead the dough vigorously, adding a little more water if necessary, until the dough is smooth and elastic. Roll the dough into a ball and place in a greased bowl, covered, for about 1 hour until it has doubled in bulk.

- While the dough is rising, dice the Mozzarella into ½-inch cubes.

- Preheat the oven to 500°. On a floured work surface roll out the dough to a ½-inch thickness. Work the dough with your hands until you form a 12-inch circle. Make small indentations with your fingers all over the dough. Layer on the cheese and then the tomatoes. Add the salmon and drizzle with the olive oil. Bake for 10 minutes. Just before the pizza is done, add the arugula and return the pizza to the oven just until it wilts.

YIELD: 1 12- TO 14-INCH PIZZA.

The baked spaghetti (see recipe on page 42) rests on a windowsill at the Belvedere Caruso, with a view of the San Giovanni del Toro church across the way.

The Belvedere Caruso

Baked-Spaghetti-and-Mozzarella-Stuffed Green Peppers

You have the option of peeling the skins from the peppers or not. I have left the hotel's version here, but I have made this with the skins on and I like it just as much.

4	green bell peppers, with bottoms that allow them to sit upright
¾	cup olive oil, plus more for sprinkling, divided
2	cloves garlic, chopped
2	large, ripe, red plum tomatoes, cut into quarters
2	tablespoons chopped fresh basil
½	teaspoon salt
½	pound spaghetti
	Grated Parmesan cheese
1	cup shredded Mozzarella cheese
¼	cup seasoned breadcrumbs or more for sprinkling
½	cup chicken broth for basting

- Preheat the oven to 375°. Clean the peppers and remove the tops and seeds. Blend 3 tablespoons of the olive oil with a little salt and rub the oil onto the outside of the peppers. Place the peppers in the oven, turning them continuously for several minutes, just so that the skins will come off easily. Remove the peppers from the oven and set them aside. Turn the oven down to 350°.
- In a large skillet, sauté the garlic and the remaining olive oil until the garlic turns golden. Add the tomatoes, half of the basil, and salt. Cook over low heat for about 15 minutes, until the tomatoes are tender.
- Meanwhile, cook the spaghetti in boiling salted water until *al dente,* about 7 minutes (do not overcook). Drain and add to the tomatoes. Add Parmesan cheese to taste.
- Peel the peppers. Stuff each evenly with the spaghetti and tomatoes, followed by the Mozzarella cheese. Place into an oiled glass baking dish and sprinkle the peppers with the breadcrumbs, remaining basil, and a little olive oil. Bake for 15 minutes or until the peppers are cooked, basting often with chicken broth to keep the dish moist.

YIELD: 4 SERVINGS

Le Sirenuse

Pennette with Mozzarella and Basil in a Tomato Sauce

2	pounds ripe red tomatoes
¼	cup extra virgin olive oil
1	clove garlic, chopped
	Salt and pepper
1	small bunch fresh basil, chopped, plus more for garnish
1½	pounds pennette
8	ounces Mozzarella cheese
	Parmesan cheese

- Peel the tomatoes and cut them into a ½-inch dice. Set aside.
- Heat the olive oil in a nonstick skillet and add the garlic, cooking until the garlic has turned golden. Add the tomatoes and season with salt and pepper. Add the basil. Bring the mixture to a gentle boil over low heat. Cook at a slow rolling boil for 15 to 20 minutes.

- Cook the pasta in boiling salted water for about 20 minutes or until *al dente.*
- Just before the tomato sauce is finished cooking, add the Mozzarella and the Parmesan cheese and more fresh basil to taste.
- Add the pasta to the pan and mix together. Serve immediately.

YIELD: 6 SERVINGS

Grand Hôtel Cocumella

Tubettini with Mussels in Parmesan-Cheese Baskets

Tubettini or tubetti are very small tubelike pasta, most often used in Italian soups. The pasta shape is widely available in the United States. But you may use any tiny pasta for this interesting and unusual appetizer.

BASKETS:

2½	cups grated Parmesan cheese

FILLING:

1	tablespoon olive oil
1	clove garlic
2	pounds mussels
1	cup water
2	cups tubettini pasta
1	tablespoon Pecorino cheese
2	tablespoons minced fresh basil, plus more for garnish
	Parmesan cheese for garnish

Positano beach scene

- Make the baskets. Use a 6-inch nonstick skillet and cover the bottom with a heavy layer of the Parmesan cheese (using a little more than ½ cup at a time), spreading it out evenly as you are going to form the cheese into a crêpe. Watch the cheese carefully as you cook it over low heat, making sure it does not stick to the pan. When the cheese turns golden, remove it from the pan and form it over the bottom of a glass, shaping it into a basket. Leave the crêpe hanging over the glass until it hardens and cools. Repeat to make 4 baskets.
- In a small skillet, heat the olive oil and sauté the garlic until it turns golden. Add the mussels and the water. Cook over medium-high, adding a little more water if necessary.
- Meanwhile, boil the pasta until *al dente.* Remove the mussels from the shells. Discard the shells and return the mussels to the skillet. Drain the pasta and add it to the skillet. Add the Pecorino cheese and the basil. Remove from the heat.
- Fill each basket, dividing the mussels evenly among them. Sprinkle with more chopped basil and Parmesan cheese.

YIELD: 4 SERVINGS

Le Sirenuse

Spaghetti alle Vongole (Spaghetti with Clams)

The clams make for a wonderful broth or sauce in this traditional Campania recipe from a grand hotel. Prepare this recipe at least three hours in advance. A variation of this recipe is to remove the clams from the shells just before serving and mince them before adding them back to the frying pan. I love this sprinkled with lots of Parmesan cheese.

2½	pounds fresh clams
½	cup extra virgin olive oil
2	cloves garlic
	Cayenne pepper
¼	cup chopped Italian (flat-leaf) parsley
1½	pounds spaghetti

- Let the clams soak in cool, salted water for 2 hours. Rinse in cool water after soaking, ensuring that only the live ones remain. Set aside.
- Heat the olive oil in a frying pan, and add the garlic, cooking until browned. Stir in cayenne pepper to taste. Add the clams to the frying pan, covering the pan with a lid, allowing the clams to steam open (about 3 to 5 minutes). Remove the clams from the pan and pass the sauce in the pan through a cheesecloth to eliminate any sand or impurities. Return the clams to the saucepan. Add the parsley and cook for another 2 to 3 minutes.
- In a large stockpot, boil the pasta in salted water until tender. Strain the spaghetti and add to the frying pan with the clams and sauce. Mix together before serving.

YIELD: 6 SERVINGS

Wine Suggestion

A dry, balanced sparkling wine such as this one, can cut through and harmonize with the various flavors and textures found in the Fettucine Pomodoro with Shellfish recipe. Chandon Brut Cuvée is a refreshing and elegant accompaniment to any fish, vegetable, or meat dish.

Arsenale Restaurant

Fettucine Pomodoro with Shellfish

Combine the shellfish as you wish in this recipe. Here, it calls for mussels, clams, and shrimp. You may wish to serve it instead with any combination or even just one of the fish.

¼	cup olive oil
3	cloves garlic, minced
1	dozen prawns or shrimp
½	pound shrimp

½	cup coarsely chopped Italian parsley
1	dozen each: mussels, littleneck clams, and cherrystone clams
1½	cups cherry tomatoes, cut in half
	Salt and pepper
1	pound fettucine

- Add the olive oil to a sauté pan and heat. Add the garlic, prawns, shrimp, and half of the parsley. Sauté 1 minute over medium-high heat. Add the mussels and clams and sauté on high for 2 minutes or until the clams open. Add the cherry tomatoes and salt and pepper to taste. Cook for 3 minutes more. Set aside and keep warm.
- Cook the fettucine and drain. Add the pasta to the sauté pan, stirring to incorporate. Transfer to a serving platter and garnish with the remaining parsley.

YIELD: 4 SERVINGS

Grand Hôtel Cocumella

Pasta and Walnut Cream Sauce in a Parmesan Cheese Bowl

Use your favorite homemade pasta recipe (or see page 183) and make any flat-noodle pasta at least ½-inch wide. Pour on this nutty butter sauce and serve in the unique basket made of grated Italian cheese.

SAUCE:

½	cup (1 stick) butter
1	cup chopped walnuts, plus ½ cup chopped for garnish
¼	cup demi-glace (or see recipe for Quick Brown Sauce, page 185)

The spaghetti with clams (in large bowl); the eggplant (see recipe on page 38); and the meatballs (see recipe on page 50) poolside at Le Sirenuse in Positano

2	cups heavy cream
¼	cup Parmesan cheese or more to taste
2	teaspoons freshly chopped basil or more to taste

BOWL:

| 1 | cup grated Parmesan cheese |

- Heat the butter in a small, nonstick skillet. Add the walnuts and sauté for 1 minute. Add the brown sauce, heavy cream, and the Parmesan cheese. Cook for 5 minutes to thicken and heat through. Set aside and keep warm.
- Bring a pot of water to a boil and cook the pasta until *al dente*. Meanwhile, make the Parmesan cheese bowls.
- In the bottom of a small nonstick pan, spread ¼ cup of the Parmesan cheese in a circular pattern. Cook over medium-high heat until the cheese bubbles and browns. Carefully remove the solid piece of cheese (it will harden quickly) and shape into a small cup. Repeat to get four cups. Pour the walnut sauce into each cup and the drained pasta around the cup. Garnish with basil.

YIELD: 4 SERVINGS

Arsenale Restaurant

Orange Roughy Flambé with Pink Peppercorns and Porcini Mushrooms

At Arsenale, they make this with a fish called El Dorado. But here, we have substituted with what is more available and is a fine fish. Not only is this dish a cinch to prepare, but it is light in texture and calories. Orange roughy, which has hit American shores from New Zealand, has a mild taste that contrasts wonderfully with the sweetness of the brandy and the tang of pink peppercorns.

Wine Suggestion

Simi Sauvignon Blanc

has the character and structure to stand up to this multi-flavored orange roughy dish.

2	6-ounce orange roughy filets
	All-purpose flour
	Salt and pepper
2	tablespoons butter
1	small onion, minced
1	tablespoon pink peppercorns, plus more for garnish
2	tablespoons all-purpose flour
¼	cup Italian parsley
¼	cup diced porcini mushrooms
2	tablespoons brandy
½	cup fish broth
	Boston lettuce
	Parmesan cheese

- Season the fish with salt and pepper and rub lightly with flour. Heat the butter in a small skillet over medium-high heat. Add the onion and sauté 1 minute. Add the peppercorns and then the fish and cook 2 minutes on each side or until lightly browned.
- Add 1 tablespoon of the parsley, followed by the mushrooms. Then, add the brandy and flame the mixture. When the flames die down, add half of the fish broth. Turn the roughy again. Add the remaining stock.
- Set some lettuce onto 2 individual serving plates. Remove the fish and mushrooms to the plates, pouring the pan juices over them. Garnish with more peppercorns. Serve with Parmesan cheese.

YIELD: 2 SERVINGS

Arsenale Restaurant

Citrus Risotto with Shrimp and Prosciutto

Risotto is like enjoying a dish of pasta, and it has the same potential as its starchy cousin in terms of preparations. Here, it is combined with fish and ham and a refreshing blend of fresh lemon and orange. Risotto utilizes short-grain rice, which is more tedious to cook than long-grain. You must stir the mixture constantly, adding liquids slowly, until the rice is *al dente.* That usually takes a total of 25 to 30 minutes.

½	**cup (1 stick) butter**
1	**medium onion, diced**
1	**tablespoon lemon zest**
2	**tablespoons orange zest**
2	**tablespoons Prosciutto, diced**
8	**ounces baby shrimp, peeled and cut into ½-inch pieces**
1½	**cups Arborio or short-grain rice, parboiled**
¼	**cup white wine**
1	**tablespoon lemon juice**
2-3	**cups fish stock**
	Salt and pepper
2	**tablespoons or more Parmesan cheese**

- Melt the butter in a large saucepan. Add the onion and sauté. Add the lemon and orange zests, the Prosciutto, shrimp, and rice, and stir continuously over medium-high heat. Add the white wine and the lemon juice. Stir well. Add 1 cup of stock (or enough to almost cover the rice mixture.) Stir until all of the liquids are absorbed. Cook 15 minutes, stirring constantly, adding more stock until the rice is tender but *al dente.* Season to taste with salt and pepper. Stir in the Parmesan cheese.

YIELD: 4 SERVINGS

Risotto at the Arsenale Restaurant

Stuffed Calamari Caruso

We also ate squid when I was growing up, but usually on a Friday night or holidays. My grandmother filled the fish with all sorts of stuffings. This one from Campania is not unlike some of the fillings she used to make. We only used the fish cavity, not the tentacles, so I have adapted this recipe the same way.

5	calamari, cleaned
¾ -1	cup seasoned breadcrumbs
½	cup chopped Italian parsley
4	cloves garlic, 3 of them minced, 1 coarsely chopped
2	anchovy filets, chopped
¼	cup small capers
	Salt
4	tablespoons olive oil
½	cup white wine

- Dice I calamaro and mix it with the breadcrumbs, half the parsley, the minced garlic, anchovies, capers, and salt to taste. (Add more breadcrumbs if desired.) Stuff each calamari evenly with this filling. Fasten with toothpicks.
- In a medium skillet, heat the olive oil and sauté the chopped garlic until it turns golden (do not brown). Add the wine, the stuffed calamari, and the remaining parsley. Cook for about 3 minutes or until the alcohol has evaporated. Add I cup of hot water and simmer the calamari over a low flame for 30 minutes.

YIELD: 4 SERVINGS

Braciole of Tenderloin in a Tomato and Wine Sauce

Braciole is the Italian word for roulade, and as I was growing up, many a braciole ended up at our table. My mother had a particular fondness for rolled meat and used to put it in the tomato sauce, which caused the sauce to be wonderfully favored with the meat, as the meat cooked tender. This braciole is simply coated with Parmesan cheese and minced parsley, rolled, and cooked in a sauce. It is served as an appetizer, but add pasta to the sauce, and you could turn this into a meal.

Wine Suggestion

AZIANO

CHIANTI CLASSICO

RUFFINO

This medium-bodied Chianti from the Tuscan Estates of Ruffino is just right for the Braciole of Tenderloin in a Tomato and Wine Sauce.

BRACIOLE:

8	slices (½-inch thick) sirloin, pounded to ¼-inch thickness
½	cup freshly grated Parmesan cheese
¼	cup Italian parsley, minced
	Salt and pepper

SAUCE:

2	tablespoons olive oil
1	medium onion, minced
3	cloves garlic, finely chopped
½	cup white wine
16	ounces canned Italian tomatoes, chopped

- Cover each piece of meat with 1 tablespoon of Parmesan and 1 teaspoon of parsley. Season with salt and pepper. Roll each slice of meat, fastening it with a toothpick, locking it in by threading the toothpick twice through the meat.
- Prepare the sauce by heating the olive oil in a medium saucepan over medium heat. Add the onions and the garlic and sauté until transluscent. Add the braciole and sauté on all sides until browned. Pour in the wine and simmer for 5 minutes. Add the tomatoes and cover, simmering for 30 minutes.
- Place 2 rolls on each individual serving plate and top with the sauce.

YIELD: 4 SERVINGS

Villa Cimbrone and its extensive gardens provide a delightful walking spot for those who have enjoyed a filling meal at the Belvedere Caruso in Ravello.

Arsenale Restaurant

Baked Red Snapper with Asparagus and Vegetable Medley

2	pounds whole red snapper
3	small potatoes, peeled and diced
1	medium carrot, cut julienne
1	medium zucchini, cut julienne
4	asparagus stalks, blanched and cut in half lengthwise
1	cup cherry tomatoes, cut in half
	Salt and pepper
1	clove garlic, minced
½	cup olive oil
½	cup water

* Preheat the oven to 375°. Place the snapper in a 9x13-inch baking pan. Add the potatoes, carrots, zucchini, asparagus, and cherry tomatoes. Season all with salt and pepper and sprinkle evenly with the garlic. Drizzle with the olive oil and then add the water. Bake 25 minutes or until the vegetables are tender.

YIELD: 2 SERVINGS

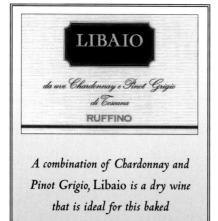

Wine Suggestion

LIBAIO

da uve Chardonnay e Pinot Grigio di Toscana

RUFFINO

A combination of Chardonnay and Pinot Grigio, Libaio is a dry wine that is ideal for this baked red snapper dish.

Le Sirenuse

Meatballs Pignoli with Raisins in Tomato Sauce

Adding *pignoli* or pine nuts and raisins to a *polpette* or meatball recipe was foreign even to this thoroughbred Italian-American. However, I was willing to give it a try and I am glad I did. This is a nice change from the standard meatball recipe, with the sweet taste of the raisins and earthy taste of the pine nuts. But that is why this book and the show are called *World Class Cuisine*—a little twist of some intriguing, not offensive, ingredient, and out comes a lot of magic for a gourmet touch that is still easy to do.

You may also cook these meatballs under a broiler, turning until golden brown. This will eliminate the steps and ingredients for frying the meatballs. Serve as an appetizer or as a main course.

2	slices soft white bread
1½	pounds ground sirloin
2	tablespoons chopped Italian parsley
2	large eggs
½	cup grated Parmesan cheese

1	clove garlic, minced
	Salt and pepper
½	cup dark raisins
½	cup pine nuts
	All-purpose flour for frying
1	cup sunflower oil
¼	cup olive oil
1	medium onion, finely diced
1	pound peeled fresh ripe tomatoes, seeds removed, and tomato cut into ½-inch dice
¼	cup tomato paste

The Meatballs Pignoli at Le Sirenuse

- Soak the white bread in enough water to cover, just until drenched, a few minutes.
- In a large bowl, mix together the meat, bread, parsley, eggs, Parmesan, garlic, and salt and pepper to taste. Mix thoroughly with your hands, making sure to break up the bread and mix evenly throughout the meat mixture. Work in the raisins and pignoli.
- Form the meat mixture into 1- to 1½-inch balls or desired meatball size. Dip the meatballs lightly in all-purpose flour. Heat the sunflower oil in a deep nonstick frying pan. Fry the meatballs until golden brown.
- In a separate skillet, heat the olive oil and sauté the onion until golden. Add the tomatoes and the tomato paste, and cook for about 15 to 20 minutes. Add the meatballs to the sauce and cook for another 10 minutes.

YIELD: 4 SERVINGS

Night falls on the cliff-side town of Positano.

Le Sirenuse

Poached Rockfish Stewed in Tomatoes and White Wine

You may use a variety of fish with this recipe including sea bass and red snapper. At Le Sirenuse, they use a local scorpion fish. The soft flesh of some varieties of rockfish, like the scorpion fish, requires a gentler cooking method, preferably baked or poached.

¼	cup extra virgin olive oil
1	clove garlic
2	pounds rockfish filets
¾	cup white wine
½	cup freshly chopped tomatoes
1	tablespoon chopped parsley
	Salt
½	cup boiling water

- Heat the olive oil in a large frying pan and sauté the garlic clove over medium heat until it turns golden. Remove from the oil and add the seafood, browning it carefully on all sides. Add the white wine and allow it to reduce until it evaporates, about 5 minutes.
- Add the tomatoes and parsley, and season with salt. Add the water and cover the pan, cooking over medium heat for about 15 minutes more. (Be careful not to overcook the fish.) Remove the cover and keep the fish simmering until most of the liquid evaporates.

YIELD: 4 SERVINGS

Grand Hôtel Cocumella

Toasted Almond-and-Chocolate Tart

Just look at the size of this recipe. It's obvious how easy it is. But the taste is not so obvious, and yet this flourless chocolate tart is a winner.

1	cup sugar
1	cup (2 sticks) butter
4	eggs
1	cup toasted chopped almonds
4	ounces quality dark chocolate, melted

- Preheat the oven to 350°. Whip together the sugar and the butter until smooth. Add the eggs and the almonds. Mix all of these ingredients and then fold in the chocolate.
- Pour the mixture into a greased and floured 9-inch cake pan and bake for 1 hour or until tester inserted comes clean. (Check after 50 minutes.)

YIELD: 8 SERVINGS

The Belvedere Caruso

Lemon-and-Ricotta Cheesecake

The Italians make their rich but lightly textured cheesecakes with Ricotta cheese, especially in Campania where they make their own Ricotta. This version is a classic cheesecake, perfect with almost any Italian meal you serve. The combination of the sweet, shortcrust pastry and the Ricotta makes for a delicious contrast. Feel free to add a seasoning of vanilla extract or cinnamon to the filling.

PASTRY:

2	cups all-purpose flour
¾	cup sugar
¼	teaspoon baking soda
3	medium eggs, beaten
¾	cup butter, cut into pieces
	Grated zest of 1 lemon

FILLING STEP 1:

3	medium eggs, beaten
⅔	cup sugar
5	tablespoons all-purpose flour
2	cups milk

FILLING STEP 2:

1½	cups Ricotta
⅓	cup candied citrus peel, chopped

FILLING STEP 3:

5	medium eggs
½	cup sugar
	Grated zest of 1 lemon

ASSEMBLY:

Egg wash
Confectioners' sugar for dusting

- Make the pastry. Mix together the flour, sugar, and baking soda. Make a well in the center and add the eggs, the butter, and the lemon peel, mixing it all in with your hands. Set the dough aside.
- Make the custard filling by mixing together the eggs, the sugar, and the flour in a large bowl. Boil the milk in a large saucepan. When the milk just begins to boil, add the dry flour mixture into the saucepan slowly, stirring continuously. Return the saucepan to a low heat, cooking the mixture gently until it thickens, stirring constantly. Allow the mixture to cool completely.
- When the custard has cooled, preheat the oven to 350°. Add the ingredients for step 2 by mixing the Ricotta and the candied peel and adding to the custard. Set aside.
- In a separate bowl, complete the filling with step 3. Beat together the eggs and sugar until smooth. Beat into Ricotta cheese-custard mixture and stir in the lemon peel. (You now have one big filling.)
- Divide the pastry in half. Roll out one half and line a 9-inch greased springform pan. Pour in the filling. Roll out the remaining half of the dough and arrange atop the filling, making sure to cover the filling well with the dough. Brush the top with an egg wash so that it browns nicely. Bake 2 hours or until a tester inserted comes clean.
- Remove the cheesecake from the oven and allow it to cool for at least 6 hours. Remove the cake from the pan and dust with confectioners' sugar.

YIELD: 8 TO 10 SLICES

Arsenale Restaurant

Granita di Limone

Growing up in the Bronx, we had many ethnic pockets surrounding where I played and went to school. Just up the street from our house, a small deli carried a soothing, cool sweet for a summer's day—real Italian ices in a variety of flavors. The tradition of Italian ices actually began in Sicily. According to legend, when the Arabs occupied Sicily, they ate the snow off Mount Etna, flavoring it with lemon juice, during the hot weather. Today, sweet ice is sought after by the Italians all summer, at all times of day. You may serve this as a palate pleaser between courses or with dessert.

2	cups water
1½	cups sugar
	Zest from 1 lemon
1¼	cups fresh lemon juice
	Lemon halves for garnish

- Bring the water to a boil in a medium saucepan. Add the sugar and the zest and stir well. Stir while boiling until the sugar dissolves. While the water boils, add the lemon juice. Remove from the heat and stir for about 5 minutes. Strain the mixture into a heat-proof bowl. Freeze for at least 1 hour, stirring every 5 to 10 minutes. The mixture will be very slushy. Ladle into dessert dishes. Garnish with lemon halves.

YIELD: 4 SERVINGS

Lemon groves climb the steep hillsides of the Amalfi coast in great abundance, and fruit vendors—such as Vincenzo DeLucia in Positano—sell the huge fruit at nearly every bend in the narrow cliff road.

Zeppole on a balcony at the Belvedere Caruso

The Belvedere Caruso

Zeppole

The preparing of zeppole, or Italian dough-nuts, is a festive sight. The small hollow circles of sticky dough cook up like soft pillows when they hit hot oil. Sprinkling the doughnuts with powdered sugar or colorful sprinkles as they do at the Belvedere Caruso adds to the merriment of making zeppole, which originated in Campania.

2	tablespoons butter
2	cups water
½	cup all-purpose flour
1	egg yolk
	Peanut oil for frying
½	cup sugar
½	cup honey
	Colored sprinkles, colored sugar, or confectioners' sugar

- Heat the butter over medium-high heat in a small saucepan. Add the water when the butter is melted and mix. Gradually stir in the flour while heating the water. Stir until thickened, about 5 minutes. Remove from the heat and let cool enough to handle.
- Place the dough on a work surface and spread the dough to make a well in the center. (You may wish to butter your hands a little to work easier with the dough.) Add the egg yolk to the well and knead to incorporate. The dough will be sticky. Form the dough into a ball.
- Flour the work surface and divide the dough into fifths. Roll each piece into a ½-inch (diameter) wide rope. Cut evenly into 6 lengths. Form a loop or a ring with each length. Press the ends together to secure.
- In a large frying pan, pour enough of the peanut oil to cover the rings. Place over high heat. Place each ring in the hot oil. Do not crowd. Fry until golden brown. Place on a plate with paper towels to drain well. Dip the rings into sugar and then into honey. Decorate with sprinkles, colored sugar, or confectioners' sugar.

YIELD: 16 TO 20 DOUGHNUTS

Grand Hôtel Cocumella

Sweet-Ricotta-and-Cinnamon Pie (Neopolitan Easter Pie)

Although it is served most often during Easter time, this lattice-topped dessert is served all year long and is considered to be the best known of all desserts from the Naples area. The pie recipe, with changes and modifications, dates to the fourteenth century and when you make it today, you will find that its superb texture and creamy taste is a hit with your guests. Start this dessert two days ahead of time in order to soak and cook the barley as described in the method.

BARLEY PREPARATION:

1	cup dried barley, soaked in water for 2 days (Change water often)
2	cups whole milk
	Finely grated zest of ½ lemon
½	lemon
⅛	teaspoon salt
½	teaspoon cinnamon
½	teaspoon vanilla extract
	Finely grated zest of ½ orange

PASTRY:

1½	cups all-purpose flour
½	cup sugar
½	cup (1 stick) butter
3	large egg yolks
⅛	teaspoon salt

FILLING:

4	egg whites
1¼	cups Ricotta cheese
1¼	cups sugar
4	egg yolks
¼	cup orange flower water
½	cup diced candied orange peel

ASSEMBLY:

	Egg wash
	Confectioners' sugar

- Start this recipe at least 6 hours before serving. Drain the soaked barley and cook the grain in a small saucepan with the milk, adding the grated lemon peel and half of a lemon with the salt. Simmer this, covered, over low heat for 4 hours. Remove from the heat and stir in the cinnamon, vanilla, and the orange peel.
- While the barley cooks, prepare the crust. Mix together the flour, sugar, butter, 3 egg yolks, and salt until a smooth ball of dough is formed. Cover with a clean cloth and refrigerate for 1 hour.
- Meanwhile, beat the egg whites until stiff peaks form. Set aside. Blend together the Ricotta, sugar, 4 egg yolks, orange flower water, the candied peel, and the cooked barley. Fold in the beaten egg whites.
- When the dough is ready, remove it from the refrigerator. Preheat the oven to 350°. Divide the chilled dough in half, rolling each half out to fit a 9-inch cake pan, pressing the pastry into the base of the pan and up the sides. Pour in the cheese filling.
- Cut the remaining dough into long ½-inch-wide strips and arrange them in lattice fashion (crisscross) over the filling. Brush the top with egg wash. Bake for 45 minutes or until the cake is set and the crust golden. Serve warm, dusted with lots of confectioners' sugar.

YIELD: 8 SERVINGS

The garden terrace at the Grand Hotel Cocumella in Sorrento is the setting for the Sweet-Ricotta-and-Cinnamon Pie.

EMILIA-ROMAGNA

— ❦ ❦ ❦ —

While Music Plays and Poppies Bloom, the Cheese Ages and the Nectar Flows

Every minute of just about every day, the pasta women known as the *sfogliatrice* in Emilia-Romagna hand-roll dough into paper-thin strips for the region's famous *tagliatelle*, or they fasten dough into the "navel of Venus," known here as tortellini. And the beat of the rolling pin goes on, for any one of dozens of pasta shapes that go to the daily market.

Meanwhile, the world's most famous grating cheese, Parmigiano-Reggiano, ages quietly under the supervision of caretakers, who check the cheese wheels for ripening with the aid of a gimlet, just as it has been done for some seven centuries.

Elsewhere, the region's famous Parma ham is readied for production and the Trebbiano grape is harvested and aged in wooden barrels for the pungent sweet nectar that is *aceto balsemico* or balsamic vinegar. Giuseppe Verdi and Arturo Toscanini would be proud of their birthplace with all of its culinary compassion, while their music plays on in the region's packed theaters and opera houses.

Both the Ravioli Florentine and the Polenta with Boar Stew (see recipes on pages 63 and 62) in the dining room, Al Vecchio Convento (meaning "At the Old Convent")

Welcome to Emilia-Romagna, home to Italy's culinary capital, Bologna, where bolognese sauce was born as well as lasagne and tortellini. Located in northern Italy, just south of Venice at the cuff of the boot, Emilia-Romagna is a prosperous farming region that produces an elaborate and bountiful magnanimous cuisine. Nobility lived here for centuries, giving the area both a healthy patronage of the arts and its culinary beginnings. Emilia and Romagna are joined together by their cuisine and by a road, the Via Emilia, but the region has had a fragmented history. The eastern or Romagna area has looked to Rome for art and political persuasion and Emilia (from Bologna to Piacenza on the west), has had more of a sense of rebellion and self-government.

Today, Emilians and Romagnolans spend hours discussing dishes and food, their most important topic after love and before music. What they put on their table is, first of all, fresh flowers, and they may be the vermillion poppies that grow widely here. Rice is a popular first course (*i primi piatti*) or pasta, which in Emilia-Romagna is often creatively filled with a mixture such as Ricotta, spinach, and sugar beets; pumpkin, Parmesan, and potato; and mushrooms, mustard, chestnuts, and carrots, to mention only a few combinations. For the second course, or *i secondi*, the ever-present veal is often served as a cutlet. *Costoletta alla bolognese* is a baked dish stuffed with cheese and truffles, dipped in breadcrumbs and covered with a layer of ham and cheese and usually tomato sauce.

Al Vecchio Convento

Zucchini Fondue with Truffles

Chef Giovanni Cameli has a passion for cheese, especially when he can melt it and serve it with the truffles he personally hunts with his dog. This recipe is a great winter dish because it is warm and hearty and would be great served in front of a fire. But it is also great to serve during summer on the cool patio when the zucchini is so ripe and fresh and plentiful.

¼	cup (½ stick) butter, divided
1	large zucchini, cut into thin strips
1	pound Fontina cheese, cut into ½-inch cubes or shredded
1	cup whole milk, heated, plus 2 teaspoons
3	egg yolks
1	black truffle or other wild mushroom
	Crusty bread for dipping, cut into bite-size pieces

- In a medium sauté pan, heat 3 tablespoons of the butter over medium-high heat. When hot, add the zucchini and sauté for 3 minutes. Set aside.
- In a large skillet, add the remaining butter and melt over medium-high heat, whisking in the cheese and ¼ cup of the milk. Slowly whisk in more milk as the cheese melts.
- Meanwhile, whisk the egg yolks in a bowl, along with about 2 teaspoons of the milk, whisking constantly as you pour the egg yolks into the melting cheese. Stir until combined but do not overmix or the eggs will curdle.
- Stir in the sautéed zucchini. Remove the fondue immediately from the heat and transfer to a serving platter. Serve with the crusty bread.

YIELD: 4 SERVINGS

Al Vecchio Convento

Tagliatelle with Spinach-and-Pancetta Sauce

Emilia-Romagna brims with ancient tradition, and at sixteenth-century banquets in Bologna, this pasta accompanied poultry and meats. In this modern-day version, Chef Giovanni Cameli chooses an Italian bacon or ham—pancetta—and spinach to complement the time-honored pasta. The chef buys his spinach from an Italian woman, who at ninety years old still runs her produce farm. Tagliatelle is a long, flat, ribbon pasta, cut just under ⅜-inch wide, if you follow the Bologna rule. Tagliatelle is a versatile pasta that goes well with light or heavy sauces.

PASTA:

4	eggs
4	cups all-purpose flour
⅛	teaspoon salt or more to taste

SAUCE:

¼	cup olive oil
8	ounces pancetta
2	cups baby spinach leaves, chopped
	Salt and pepper
1	small dried chili pepper, chopped
3	medium ripe red tomatoes, diced
	Parmesan cheese for garnish

Chef Giovanni Cameli and his dog, hunting for precious truffles—the elusive and most-prized of all edible mushrooms—near Portico di Romagna

- Mix the pasta ingredients in a large bowl and form into a dough, kneading until smooth and elastic. Pass through a pasta machine or roll out to ⅛-inch thickness. Cut into 8-inch-long by ⅜-inch-wide strips.
- Heat the olive oil in a large saucepan over medium-high heat. Add the pancetta and cook until browned. Add the spinach and season with salt and pepper. (Watch the salt as the pancetta is highly seasoned.) Add the chili peppers and tomatoes and continue to cook for about 2 minutes on medium heat.
- Meanwhile, cook the pasta in a large pot of boiling water for about 2 minutes or until *al dente.* Drain the pasta and add it to the pancetta and spinach. Toss well to coat the tagliatelle. Sprinkle with the grated cheese and serve immediately.

YIELD: 4 SERVINGS

Wine Suggestion

This medium-bodied, full-flavored wine from the small Lodola Nuova vineyard in the picturesque Tuscan hill town of Montepulciano, produces flavors reminiscent of anise and red berries to complement the tagliatelle.

Wine Suggestion

RUFFINO

RISERVA DUCALE®

Chianti Classico
DENOMINAZIONE DI ORIGINE CONTROLLATA
E GARANTITA
Riserva

BOTTLED BY
I. L. RUFFINO
FONTASSIEVE · ITALIA · 126/FI

750 ml ℮   ALCOHOL
                13% BY VOL

*The Polenta with Boar Stew is
well paired with Ruffino's renowned
and richly textured* Chianti Classico
Riserva Ducale Gold Label, *a
wine that displays a deeply concentrated
ripe, black fruit character and finesse.*

Al Vecchio Convento

Polenta with Boar Stew

Polenta is a staple of northern Italy, particularly in Emilia-Romagna. The quiet, yet satisfying, taste of this cornmeal-based polenta marries well with the intensely flavored stew. Unlike many polenta recipes, this one is not baked to a solid, but rather

served with the sauce from the stew, so it tends to be more of a very thick farina or mush. If you cannot find boar, substitute with beef-stew meat.

POLENTA:

1	gallon water
	Salt
1	pound cornmeal

STEW:

¼	cup olive oil
1½	pounds boar meat, cut into 1-inch cubes
3	tablespoons all-purpose flour
	Salt and pepper
1	cup red wine
1	sprig fresh sage
2	sprigs fresh rosemary
2	sprigs fresh thyme
1	bay leaf
1	large fresh porcini mushroom, sliced
1	medium onion, minced
2	ribs celery, minced
3	medium tomatoes, diced
¼	cup water

- In a large saucepan, bring the water to a boil. Add about 2 tablespoons of salt. As the mixture boils, slowly pour in the cornmeal, stirring constantly. Stir with a whisk until thickened and then with a wooden spoon for about 15 minutes. The polenta should be thick enough that a spoon stands up in it.
- Heat the olive oil in a large sauté pan over medium heat. Add the boar and sear on each side. Sprinkle the flour over the meat and season with salt and pepper. Pour in the red wine. Tie the sage, rosemary, thyme, and bay leaf together with kitchen string and add to the sauté pan. Cook for 4 minutes and then add about ¼ cup of water. Add the vegetables to the pan. Cover and cook for 2 hours or until the

meat is fork tender. Remove the bundle of herbs and discard.

- To serve, place about half of the stew liquid onto a serving platter. Spoon the polenta on either side of the dish and add the meat to the center. Pour the remaining sauce overall and serve immediately.

———————————
YIELD: 4 SERVINGS

Al Vecchio Convento Chef Giovanni Cameli gets spinach for his tagliatelle recipe fresh from Maria Aurelia at her nearby produce farm. (See recipe on page 61.)

Al Vecchio Convento

Ravioli Florentine with Sage Butter and Truffles

Draped in a sauce of timeless fresh sage and melted butter, this stuffed pasta is ignited with the powerful flavor of Italian black truffles. At Al Vecchio Convento, Chef Giovanni Cameli enjoys truffle hunting and uses the mushroom in many of his dishes. You can find imported truffles in gourmet food boutiques. They are worth the hefty price.

FILLING:

10	ounces fresh spinach leaves, cleaned and stemmed
1	cup Ricotta cheese
½	cup freshly grated Parmesan cheese, plus more for garnish
1	egg, slightly beaten
½	teaspoon grated nutmeg
	Salt and pepper
1	pound fresh pasta dough, rolled into a large circle, ⅛-inch thick (see page 183 for recipe)
¼	cup butter
6-8	fresh sage leaves
1	large fresh truffle

- Bring a large pot of water to boil. Add the spinach and cook 2 minutes, or just until it wilts. Remove the spinach with a slotted spoon. Coarsely chop the spinach and place in a medium bowl. Add the Ricotta, Parmesan, egg, nutmeg, and the salt and pepper. Stir to mix well.
- Lay out the pasta sheet and place 1 teaspoon of the Ricotta filling in rows at 1-inch intervals. Cover only half of the pasta sheet. Fold the other half over the filling. With a pasta cutter, cut out 2-inch squares, with the filling in the center of each square.
- Fill a large saucepan with water and add salt. While waiting for the water to boil, melt the butter in a small sauté pan and add the sage. Gently coat the uncooked pasta in the butter mixture and then add the pasta to the boiling water. Cook 2 to 4 minutes until tender or *al dente.*
- Remove the stuffed pasta with a slotted spoon and place on a serving platter. Pour the sage butter over it and sprinkle with Parmesan cheese. Garnish with shaved truffle and serve immediately.

———————————
YIELD: 4 SERVINGS

Al Vecchio Convento

Herbed Lamb Chops with an Olive-and-Balsamic-Vinegar Sauce

Situated in the mountains of Emilia-Romagna, Al Vecchio Convento is surrounded by history. This small inn has exceptional food that is a nice combination of sophisticated Bolognese and country. Seasoned with an assortment of fine herbs, this lamb dish excites the palate with its bounty of textures and tastes.

1½	pounds lamb chops
2	tablespoons olive oil
	Salt and pepper
¼	cup or less all-purpose flour
½	cup white wine
½	cup chopped black olives
1	sprig fresh rosemary, leaves removed, stem discarded, plus more for garnish
3	fresh sage leaves, chopped, plus more for garnish
1	bay leaf
1	clove garlic, minced
¼	cup Italian (flat-leaf) parsley
1½	cups balsamic vinegar

* Pound the lamb chops well to flatten. Heat olive oil in a large sauté pan or skillet over a medium-high flame. Add the lamb to the pan and sprinkle with salt and pepper. Toss the meat with enough flour to cover the top of the meat and cook about 2 minutes. Turn the lamb chops over and season with salt and pepper. Sprinkle with more flour to cover and continue cooking. Add the wine and the olives, and shake the pan to prevent sticking.
* Add the herbs and garlic to the pan and then add 1 cup of the vinegar. Transfer the lamb mixture to a smaller sauté pan, and continue cooking 1 to 2 minutes, covered. Stir in the remaining vinegar and remove the lamb to a serving platter. Remove and discard the bay leaf. Pour the sauce over all and garnish with more fresh herbs.

YIELD: 4 SERVINGS

The tiny riverside village of Portico di Romagna in the heart of the Emilia-Romagna region

The herbed lamb chops, fireside in the dining room, Al Vecchio Convento

TUSCANY

❧ ❧ ❧

A 3,000-Year-Old Bean Pot Keeps on Cooking

*T*uscany is a place that, once you visit, its spirit remains with you and may even change your life. The jubilant city of Florence gives the region its metropolitan feel, but Tuscany is largely countryside, a patchwork quilt of farms and groves of olive trees that look like orderly dots on the tranquil landscape. It is almost like living a fairytale when you stay in the country, throw open the hallmark louvered wooden shutters (there is no glass in the windows of most farmhouses), and peer out at carpeted green hills enriched by the soil that still produces the essence of an old region.

The food here is about the simplest in all of Italy but possibly the most eloquent—rough but refined. It is based on bread, oil, beans, and wine, as it has been for three thousand years. The Tuscans believe in purity of flavors—no smothering of dishes in sauces and gravies. It is more important to these humble people that they taste the very soul of their food.

Locanda dell'Amorosa (loosely meaning the country inn of love or romance) is the quintessential Tuscan farm villa. The complex includes the restaurant, guest rooms, and here: the central courtyard with its chapel and a perfect spot for the Chilled Tomato Terrine to rest atop the old cistern.

Take the Tuscan bread for example. Baked in brick ovens to a crusty shell that encloses a chewy, dense interior, the *pane* is made with plain flour or the more indigenous chestnut flour that is also used for making pasta, polenta, and desserts. But the real signature of Tuscan bread is the fact that it is made without salt, so the pure taste comes through, not only in the bread, but in the rest of the meal. The wan taste acts as a foil to some of the spicier dishes and salty preserved meats. At first bite it is quite a shock to the palate but after a few slices, one begins to understand why it has been made this way for centuries. A cruet of olive oil is on the table for rubbing on the bread instead of butter.

The pallid taste of the bread also allows for the area's famous *crostini* appetizer. A variety of toppings, such as minced clams, chicken liver, onions, olive spreads, and roasted red bell peppers, are placed on slices of toasted bread.

Tuscany is also the home of Chianti wine, recognizable by the bulbous bottles in wicker baskets. I enjoy grabbing a picnic basket, going to one of the medieval towns, and looking at the landscape from atop the city walls—with bread, olives, Chianti, and the Tuscan sunshine.

Beans are another staple of the Tuscan diet. Tuscans are called *mangiafagioli* or bean eaters. White beans, or cannellini, were introduced to the region by Alessandro dé Medici in the sixteenth century and they are now an essential ingredient in many dishes—often mixed with pasta, hence the well-known *pasta e fagioli.*

Meat is also on the Tuscan menu. Its origin, cuts, and cooking techniques are characteristically Tuscan. In particular, *bistecca,* a T-bone or sirloin steak from a young steer, must be cut about one-and-one-half to two inches thick, or as they say here, as thick as the index and middle finger joined together. It then must be sprinkled generously with sea salt, grilled over charcoal, and served with a brushing of olive oil and a side of lemon wedges.

In Tuscany, much of the cooking revolves around an open hearth, an ancient method made convenient with brick hearths built into modern kitchens at eye-level. Cooks prefer to use earthenware pots and pans, as they believe these vessels draw out the food's true flavor. It is a safe bet that a bean pot simmers slowly in Tuscan farmhouses every day. The Tuscans make way for the old, producing a rustic, reverent, fiery cuisine that has all of the elements sought after in today's healthier lifestyles.

In addition to these Tuscan dietary staples, the region is rich in blueberries, chestnuts in the mountains, and trout in the streams. Wild boar is a favorite meat delicacy, as you can see in the recipes that follow—recipes that will certainly enrich your pantry at home and make you think of the joy of Tuscany.

The majestic Palazzo Pubblico casts its shadow across Il Campo (the grand piazza) in medieval Siena.

Castello di Spaltenna

Portobello Mushrooms with Garlic and Olive Oil

A friend originally introduced me to "fancying up" portobello (or you may use porcini) mushrooms with some simple ingredients and enjoying it as an appetizer. The mushroom is so delicious that people remark, "This is like biting into a steak." But of course there are far fewer calories. Castello di Spaltenna bakes the mushroom in an oven, but try bathing the mushroom caps with a vinaigrette marinade and grilling them until browned. You may sprinkle these cooked mushrooms with a little balsamic vinegar before serving.

4	medium portobello mushrooms
4	garlic cloves, minched
4	small branches Italian (flat-leaf) parsley, finely chopped
¼	cup olive oil
	Salt and pepper

- Preheat the oven to 400°. Clean the mushrooms with a clean cloth (do not wash with water). Remove the stems, leaving the cap intact. Dice the stems and add them to a bowl with the garlic, parsley, olive oil, and salt and pepper. Brush the top and underside of each cap, using up all of the mixture. Wrap each mushroom in aluminum foil and bake for 10 to 15 minutes or until heated through and tender. Cut in half if serving more people.

YIELD: 4 SERVINGS OR 8 HALF SERVINGS

Locanda dell' Amorosa

Chilled Tomato Terrine

2	tablespoons extra virgin olive oil
½	cup finely chopped leek (white part)
½	cup finely chopped celery
2	pounds fresh tomatoes, chopped into 1- to 2-inch dice
2	tablespoons tomato paste
2	tablespoons ketchup
2	tablespoons finely chopped fresh tarragon
2	tablespoons finely chopped fresh basil, plus more for garnish
5	gelatin leaves, softened in cold water
½	cup whipped cream
	Salt and pepper

- In a medium saucepan, heat the olive oil and sauté the chopped leeks and celery until translucent. Add the tomatoes and cook for 10 minutes on low heat. Add the tomato paste and the ketchup and stir into the cooked tomato mixture. Pass the mixture through a sieve.
- Add the tarragon and the basil to the tomato mixture. Fold in the gelatin leaves. Stir in the whipped cream. Season all with salt and pepper. Place the mixture in a terrine or bread pan and allow to cool in the refrigerator for several hours until set.
- Slice the chilled tomato mixture and place on the serving plate. Garnish with basil leaves. Drizzle with olive oil, if desired.

YIELD: 4 TO 6 SERVINGS

Castello di Spaltenna

Vegetable Mousse Trio with Parmesan Sauce

PARMESAN SAUCE:

1	clove garlic
1	cup Parmesan cheese
¾	cup light cream
½	cup milk
	Salt and pepper
2	egg yolks

SPINACH MOUSSE:

2½	cups coarsely chopped spinach
¾	cup heavy cream
2	eggs

FENNEL MOUSSE:

4	cups chopped fresh fennel
¾	cup heavy cream
2	eggs

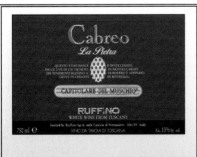

*W*ine Suggestion

This richly textured and complex Chardonnay is a perfect match for the vegetable mousse.

TOMATO MOUSSE:

	Olive oil
2	cloves garlic, chopped
4	cups chopped fresh tomatoes
¾	cup heavy cream
2	eggs

- Make the Parmesan sauce. Add the garlic, Parmesan, light cream, milk, and a sprinkling of salt and pepper to a double boiler. Cook over medium heat until the cheese is melted. Remove the mixture from the heat and whisk in the egg yolks, making sure not to let them curdle. Set aside. Preheat the oven to 325°.
- To prepare the spinach mousse, blanch the spinach in boiling water and drain. Place in a blender with the eggs and cream. Process until smooth. Place in a small ovenproof bowl. Set aside.
- To prepare the fennel mousse, boil the fennel in water until tender. Drain and place in a blender with the eggs and cream. Process until smooth. Place in a small ovenproof bowl. Set aside.
- To prepare the tomato mousse, heat the olive oil in a skillet and brown the garlic lightly. Add the tomatoes. Cook until almost all of the liquid evaporates. Place contents of skillet, cream, and eggs in the food processor and whirl until smooth. Place in a small ovenproof bowl. Set aside.
- Bake the mousses in the oven for 30 minutes or until lightly browned.
- Form each mousse into a quenelle shape (football shape) using 2 spoons, or use an ice cream scoop. For each serving, place a scoop of each flavor and a draping of sauce on a plate.

YIELD: 6 SERVINGS

Castello di Spaltenna

Mixed Tuscanese Salad with Pecorino Cheese and Walnuts

Simply double or multiply the ingredients in this recipe accordingly.

2	cups assorted baby lettuce such as arugula, endive, and watercress, coarsely shredded
1	fresh green broad bean (or substitute with 3 string beans), thinly sliced
1	spring onion (white part only), thinly sliced
½	cup Pecorino cheese, thinly shaved

Castello di Spaltenna, a medieval castle turned into a wonderful Tuscan refuge for fine dining and lodging in Gaiole-in-Chianti by Julia Scartozzoni and Chef Seamus O'Kelly

¼	cup walnut halves
2-3	tablespoons olive oil
1	tablespoon chopped Italian parsley
	Salt

- Arrange the lettuce on a large dinner plate. Sprinkle the bean slices over the lettuce. Add the onion and place the cheese shavings in the center. Top with the walnuts and drizzle with the olive oil. Sprinkle with parsley and salt to taste.

YIELD 1 SERVING

*Wine Suggestion*

The Chandon Carneros Blanc de Noirs' superb Pinot Noir and Pinot Meunier grapes from the cool Carneros district of California combine to produce a sparkling wine with the necessary fruit complexity and structure to complement the flavors in this Tuscan salad with Pecorino cheese.

Castello di Spaltenna

Ricotta-and-Herb-Stuffed Purses with Tomato and Watercress Sauces

This unusual dish from Tuscany is an appetizer in a surprising bundle making use of borage, a popular vegetable in Europe that tastes something like a cucumber.

CRÊPES:

¾	cup all-purpose flour
2	eggs
¾	cup milk

FILLING:

¾	cup Ricotta cheese
¼	cup assorted fresh herbs such as rosemary, thyme, borage, and sage
	Salt and pepper

TOMATO SAUCE:

2	tablespoons olive oil
2	large cloves garlic, peeled
3	ripe red tomatoes, chopped

WATERCRESS SAUCE:

2	tablespoons olive oil
2	red onions, thinly sliced
1	white potato, peeled and thinly sliced
1	cup watercress
¼	cup vegetable stock

ASSEMBLY:

	Fresh parsley, with stems for tying

The Ricotta and Herb-Stuffed Purses with two sauces

- Mix together the flour, eggs, and milk, making a thin crêpe batter. Heat a crêpe iron or a non-stick crêpe pan or small skillet, and make 4 crêpes, cooking until lightly browned (about 30 seconds on each side).
- Set the crêpes aside and prepare the filling. In a bowl, mix the Ricotta with the herbs. Season with salt and pepper. Set aside. Prepare the sauces, beginning with the tomato sauce.
- In a large saucepan, heat the olive oil. When hot, add the garlic and sauté until lightly browned. Add the tomato and cook over medium heat until the tomatoes are tender, about 25 minutes. Transfer the mixture to a blender and process until smooth. Set aside and keep warm. Prepare the watercress sauce.
- In a large saucepan, heat the olive oil. When the oil is hot, add the onion and sauté until translu-

cent. Add the potatoes and watercress and cook over medium heat until the potatoes are tender, about 20 minutes. Add the vegetable stock and cook over medium heat for about 10 minutes. Transfer the mixture to a blender and process until smooth. Set aside and keep warm.

- Preheat the oven to 375°. Fill the crêpe bundles. Place the crêpes on a flat surface. Spread evenly with the filling. Soften the stalks of parsley in water to use for tying the bundles. Gather the crêpe around to the center over the filling and tie with the parsley. Repeat, using all of the crêpes.
- Place the bundles on a greased baking sheet and place in the oven for about 5 minutes, or just until the bundles turn a golden brown.
- To serve, ladle the 2 sauces side by side on each individual serving plate. Place a bundle in the center and serve immediately.

YIELD: 4 SERVINGS

Certosa di Maggiano

Bread of the Saints

Tuscans are religious people and on the Feast of All Saints Day on November 1, they pay tribute to the saints with this bread. Also known as *pan coi santi* or bread with the saints, this is actually a sweet yeast bread with a peppery taste. It is dunked in red wine when it becomes hard or stale.

1	tablespoon active dry yeast
1	cup warm water (110°)
¼	cup extra virgin olive oil
1	cup walnuts, coarsely chopped
3	cups all-purpose flour
⅓	cup sugar
1	tablespoon freshly ground pepper
	Salt

- In a small bowl, proof the yeast in the water, letting it stand until dissolved and foamy, about 10 minutes. Meanwhile, in a small skillet, over very low heat, warm the olive oil and brown the nuts. Sauté gently until toasted, about 2 minutes. Remove from the heat, allowing the nuts and oil to cool completely.
- In a large bowl, combine the flour, sugar, pepper, and salt. Remove to a work surface and make a well in the center. Pour in the yeast and then the cooled nuts and oil. Using a fork, gradually work in the mixture until all of it is absorbed.
- On a lightly floured work surface, knead the dough until elastic, about 10 minutes. Shape into a ball. Transfer the dough to a lightly oiled bowl and cover with plastic wrap. Let rise at room temperature until doubled in bulk, about 2 hours.
- Turn the dough out onto a floured work surface. Punch the dough down and form into a flat oval loaf, about 1-inch thick at the center and ½-inch thick at the edges. Lightly oil a baking sheet and place the loaf onto it. Let it rise at room temperature until doubled in size, about 30 minutes. Meanwhile, preheat the oven to 400°.
- Bake the bread for about 30 minutes or until a tester inserted comes out clean. Remove the bread from the oven and let cool completely on a wire rack.

YIELD: 1 LOAF (ABOUT 6 SERVINGS)

Castello di Spaltenna

Focaccia Bread with Olives, Tomatoes, and Anchovies, or Potato-and-Celery Topping

Focaccia is Italian flat bread that is baked to a soft crust. The inn's version includes a choice of toppings, which you may add or not. Focaccia is characterized by small thumb-print indentations made in the bread during the shaping of the dough. These hold the toppings while they bake.

Chef Seamus de Pentheney O'Kelley makes his focaccia with potatoes to make the bread a bit more moist, but we cannot help thinking that it is also a tip-of-the-shamrock to his Irish heritage.

The Tuscans often simply add chopped olives to this recipe and their ubiquitous choice of herbs, particularly oregano, sage, rosemary, and thyme. Focaccia is popular all over Italy, often found in sandwich shops and bakeries. In the Liguria region they even make a sweet focaccia.

You may serve the savory bread with a hard or soft Italian cheese or enjoy it as an accompaniment to a vinaigrette salad. Focaccia is also delicious served with diced tomatoes, garlic, and herbs, run into the oven just long enough for a heaping grating of Parmigiano-Reggiano cheese to melt. In Tuscany, they also call this bread *schiacciata*.

Bake this recipe with whichever topping you wish, or no topping at all. This recipe will yield 3 14- to 16-inch focaccia breads.

DOUGH:

4	ounces yeast
2	cups warm water
8	cups all-purpose flour
4	white potatoes (1 pound), peeled and cooked until very tender, diced
1	tablespoon salt
2	cups milk
½	cup olive oil

OLIVES, TOMATOES, WITH ANCHOVIES:

4	medium tomatoes, peeled, chopped, and cooked in a skillet with a tablespoon or so of olive oil and 2 tablespoons dried oregano
1½	cups pitted olives, coarsely chopped
	Salt and pepper
12-15	anchovy filets
	Olive oil

POTATO AND CELERY TOPPING:

6	white potatoes, peeled and cooked tender
½	cup finely chopped celery
1	red onion, coarsely chopped
	Olive oil

- Preheat the oven to 375°. Dissolve the yeast in the warm water. On a work surface, make a well in the center of the flour. Pour the yeast mixture into the well. Mix in the cooked potatoes and salt and add in the milk and oil. Knead the mixture until a soft dough forms, about 10 minutes. (Add more flour to keep the dough from sticking.) Shape the dough into a loaf and then cut into 3 equal pieces. Shape each piece into an oval.
- Sprinkle the work surface with flour and roll out the dough to ½-inch thickness. Place on a sheet pan that has been brushed lightly with olive oil. Cover and let rise for about 35 minutes. Press your thumb all around the dough to make indentations and let the dough rise again

for another 30 minutes. Repeat with the remaining portions. Bake the bread for 30 minutes or until golden brown and the bread sounds hollow when tapped.

Variation with Toppings:

- Cover the rolled and thumb-printed dough with the tomatoes. Evenly spread the olives across the bread, about every 2 inches or so. Season with salt and pepper, and top with the anchovies. Let rise in a warm place for 35 minutes. Bake as directed.
- Cover the rolled and thumb-printed dough with the potatoes, then the celery and the onion. Sprinkle with salt and pepper and drizzle with olive oil. Let the dough rise for 35 minutes at room temperature. Bake as directed.

YIELD: 3 LOAVES

Wine Suggestion

The lively fresh fruit in Clivo pairs well with the flavors of the bread and tomato salad.

Panzanella (Bread-and-Tomato Salad)

Well, here it is, an ingenious combination of bread with your salad in one dish. What seems to have started as a way to use up day-old bread, this will become a favorite, especially for your summertime meals, when sun-ripened tomatoes are so plentiful.

2	cups diced stale crusty Italian bread
6	ripe tomatoes, cut into chunks
3	spring onions, thinly sliced
1½	cucumbers, peeled and thinly sliced
1	sprig fresh basil
	Salt
	Extra virgin olive oil
	Red wine vinegar

- Place the bread in a large bowl and add enough water just to cover. Soak the bread in the water for 10 minutes. Squeeze the bread between your hands to remove the water. Then rub with your palms, to form coarse crumbs.
- Collect the crumbs (make sure they are dry) and place them into a large salad bowl. Add the tomatoes, onions, and cucumbers to the breadcrumbs. Season with snips of the basil sprig, salt, and a little olive oil to coat. Toss the salad carefully with your hands. Place in the refrigerator to chill until needed. At the last moment add the vinegar and a little more oil for taste and texture.

YIELD: 4 SERVINGS

Malfatti Florentine (Spinach Dumplings)

These small ovals or dumplings of flour and cheese with spinach make a nice appetizer, or first course, but I have enjoyed them as a main course with a garden salad. You may serve the *malfatti* with either melted butter and Parmesan cheese or tomato sauce.

The focaccia bread on the steps at Castello di Spaltenna (See recipe on page 74.)

1	pound spinach, coarsely chopped
1½	cups Ricotta cheese
4	large eggs
¼	cup grated Parmesan or Pecorino Romano cheese
1	teaspoon all-purpose flour
	Salt and pepper
	Nutmeg

- In a large bowl, mix together the spinach, Ricotta, eggs, cheese, and the flour. Season with salt, pepper, and nutmeg.
- Form the mixture into balls, about ½-inch. Using a spoon, flatten each ball. Using the palm of your hand, shaping into ovals. Cook the malfatti in boiling salted water. Drain and serve with butter or even a tomato sauce.

YIELD: 4 APPETIZER SERVINGS

Castello di Spaltenna

Zucchini Flowers Stuffed with Ricotta and Thyme with a Zucchini Sauce

The blooms of the zucchini plant make wonderful appetizers, stuffed or fried lightly in olive oil and seasoned with salt and pepper, as my grandmother used to do. In most parts of America and Europe, this is a summer dish. The thyme is very prevalent in this dish, as it is one of Tuscany's premier spices.

SAUCE:

4-5	small zucchini, cut into chunks
2	tablespoons butter
	Salt and pepper

BLOSSOMS:

2	small zucchini, finely diced
3	eggs
¼	cup Parmesan cheese
3	cups Ricotta cheese
2	tablespoons freshly chopped thyme
12	zucchini flowers

* Boil the zucchini chunks in water until soft and tender, about 10 to 15 minutes. Drain well. Place in a food processor or blender and add the butter, and salt and pepper to taste. Mix slowly to obtain a puréed or thick, creamy sauce.
* Preheat the oven to 325°. In a large bowl, mix together the stuffing ingredients. (Note: You may prepare the stuffing without the fresh zucchini chunks and eggs.) Stuff the flowers evenly until all of the mixture is used up. Warm the sauce (not too hot). Bake blossoms for 10 minutes, or just until heated through. Serve 2 per plate with the sauce.

YIELD: 6 SERVINGS

The Panzanella against the elegant backdrop of the arcade at Certosa di Maggiano, a former monastery that is now an elegant country hotel and restaurant—not far outside the old city walls of Siena (See recipe on page 75.)

Certosa di Maggiano

Ribollita
(Twice-Cooked Soup)
with Beans, Cabbage,
and Vegetables

Ribollita is everywhere in Tuscany. This hearty so-called "bread soup" is boiled and then usually reboiled the next day before serving. Some ribollitas are so thick they are eaten with a fork, testing the definition of soup. Ribollita at Certosa di Maggiano is served alongside the ever-present extra virgin olive oil and a pepper mill. Thus each person gets to season the dish according to taste. The inn's ribollita is boiled only once and reboiled only if left over.

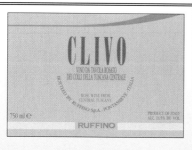

Wine Suggestion

The ripe strawberry flavor and creamy texture in the delightful dry Clivo *from Ruffino beautifully complement the Ribollitta.*

1½	cups dried cannellini beans
½	cup olive oil
2	medium onions, 1 finely chopped, the other sliced into thin rings
¼	cup tomato purée
2	carrots, thinly sliced
2	ribs celery, thinly sliced
2	ripe Italian plum tomatoes, peeled, seeded, and diced
2	leaves Swiss chard (or substitute spinach)
2	leaves purple cabbage
¼	head Savoy cabbage
	Salt and pepper
6	slices toasted, day-old Italian bread
	Onion rings

- Rinse the beans and cover with cold water (about 8 cups), bringing the beans to a boil over high heat. Turn down to a simmer and cook the beans until tender, about 2 hours.
- In a large stockpot, heat the olive oil and sauté the chopped onion until translucent. Add about 5 cups of water and the tomato purée. Add the carrots, celery, and tomatoes. Add the liquid from the cooked beans. Purée two thirds of the beans. Add them to the soup, reserving the other whole beans.
- Cut the chard and the purple and Savoy cabbages into strips. Add the cabbages to the soup. Cook, covered, for 1 hour over medium heat. Add the reserved whole cannellini beans to the soup. Add salt and pepper to taste. Cook for 10 minutes more.
- For each serving, place a slice of bread and onion rings in an individual bowl. Add the soup.

YIELD: 6 SERVINGS

The baked duck breast (see recipe on page 93) and bean soup on the grounds of La Chiusa in Montefollonico

La Chiusa

Italian Barley-and-White-Bean Soup Purée

All you need to do is start this dish a day ahead of time in order to soak the beans. The rest is a cinch and the result is a tasty soup that is actually lighter than you might guess.

8	ounces navy beans, soaked in water 24 hours
½	cup barley
¼	cup olive oil, plus more for drizzling
1	onion, peeled and thinly sliced
1	carrot, thinly sliced
1	rib celery, thinly sliced
	Salt and pepper
1	large ripe red tomato, diced

- Cover the soaked beans with water in a saucepan. Cook the beans over medium heat until tender, about 1 hour.
- About 30 minutes into the cooking of the beans, fill a 4-quart saucepan half full of salted water. Add the barley and cook until tender over medium heat, about 30 minutes.
- When the beans are done, drain them and set them aside. Heat the olive oil in a medium saucepan and sauté the onion, carrot, celery. Cook the vegetables over high heat until they are very tender, about 15 minutes. Season with salt and pepper.
- Drain the cooked beans and place them in a pan with the tender vegetables. Add the tomato and cook 30 minutes more. Transfer the vegetables and the beans to a food processor. Strain the barley and add to the processor. Purée until the mixture is smooth. If the soup is too thick, slowly add a little more water and return it to the stove to heat for 5 minutes. Ladle the soup into bowls and drizzle with olive oil.

YIELD: 4 SERVINGS

Certosa di Maggiano

Pasta e Ceci alla Toscana (Pasta and Chickpeas Tuscanese)

An easy-to-prepare dish, this is also nutritious and its method of cooking typical of Tuscan style. You can make the dish with any small pasta. They make their own at Certosa di Maggiano.

1	cup dried chickpeas
1	rib celery, finely chopped
4	small carrots, finely chopped
1	onion, finely chopped
2	cups chicken stock, or more
1	sprig rosemary
1	cup uncooked pasta
	Parmesan cheese
	Olive oil

- Soak the chickpeas in cold water overnight. Next day, cook the chickpeas with the celery, carrots, and onion, in the chicken stock, for about 1 to 1½ hours or until the chickpeas are tender.
- When cooked, scoop out about two thirds of the chickpeas and place them in a blender. (It is fine if some of the vegetables are scooped out with the peas.) Purée the chickpeas. In a medium saucepan, cook the puréed chickpeas over a high flame and add a sprig of rosemary. bring to the boil, stirring to prevent sticking. Add the whole chickpeas and the pasta and cook over medium heat, stirring frequently, until the pasta is cooked *al dente*. Flavor with the cheese and a few drops of olive oil.

YIELD: 4 TO 6 SERVINGS

One of Il Bottaccio's poolside dining room tables hosts the pasta-and-oysters recipe.

Il Bottaccio

Pasta Stuffed with Oysters in a Sweet Bell-Pepper Sauce

The smoky flavor of the roasted peppers and the mild taste of the oysters perfectly complement each other. The peppers give the dish its perfume and color, offering a sensual plate to set before your guests. Making the homemade pasta is worth the effort, as it makes this entrée light and easily digestible.

PASTA:

2	cups all-purpose flour
⅛	teaspoon salt
2	tablespoons olive oil
1	egg
3	egg yolks

FILLING:

12	oysters
2	tablespoons olive oil
2	tablespoons white wine
	Salt and freshly ground pepper

SAUCE:

1	yellow bell pepper
1	red bell pepper
2	tablespoons olive oil
3	tablespoons light cream
	Salt

ASSEMBLY:

	Egg wash

- In a large bowl, sift the flour with the salt. Add the oil, the whole egg, and the 3 egg yolks, and begin working the mixture from the inside, until a smooth, elastic dough is formed. Turn the dough out onto a baking sheet and let it rest for 30 minutes in the refrigerator.
- Meanwhile, make the filling. Open the oysters and remove them from their shells. Heat the olive oil in a pan and cook the oysters with the white wine and some salt and pepper until lightly browned. Remove from the heat and drain the oysters.
- Roast the peppers on a grill or in a hot oven until blackened. Remove the skins, membranes, and seeds and cut into thin strips. Set the peppers aside to make the sauce later.
- Remove the dough from the refrigerator. Roll the dough out into thin sheets (about ⅛-inch) through a pasta machine. Cut into 2-inch-long strips. Arrange the oysters on the strips, leaving 1 inch on either side. Fold each piece into thirds lengthwise. Seal by pressing lightly around each oyster. Cut into squares, as for ravioli.
- Boil the stuffed pasta in salted water until cooked *al dente*, about 5 minutes. While the pasta cooks, finish the sauce.
- Heat a skillet with the oil and sauté the roasted peppers for a few minutes. Add the cream and salt and let simmer for about 5 minutes.
- Drain the pasta and toss with the pepper sauce. Sprinkle with freshly chopped parsley and serve.

YIELD: 4 SERVINGS

Il Bottaccio

Wagon Wheels with Swordfish Ragu

The traditional ragu, usually made with beef, gets a lift to the lighter side by substituting swordfish for the beef. Ragu, or ragout, typically comprises tomatoes, beef, and vegetables. This entrée is a meal in itself.

¼	cup olive oil
¼	cup finely chopped celery
¼	cup finely chopped carrots
¼	cup diced onions
1	teaspoon dried marjoram
1	teaspoon ground sage
½	pound swordfish, minced
¼	cup chopped fresh tomatoes, seeds removed
	Salt
1	teaspoon vegetable broth or to taste, optional
½	cup white wine
1	pound wagon-wheel or other short pasta, cooked *al dente*
	Parmesan cheese

🌿 🌿 🌿

- In a large skillet, heat the olive oil and add the celery and carrots, cooking until they brown slightly. Turn the heat down. Add the onion with the marjoram and sage. Add the swordfish and turn the heat to a simmer. Cook for about 3 minutes. Add the tomatoes and season with salt and vegetable broth. Cook for another 2 minutes. Douse with the white wine and cook for about 3 minutes more or until the alcohol evaporates. Add the cooked pasta and serve with Parmesan cheese.

YIELD: 4 SERVINGS

Certosa di Maggiano

Penne with Puréed Cannellini in a Sienese Sausage-Wine Sauce

The Tuscans love their beans and especially mixing the beans with pasta. This is one hearty dish that you will serve over and over again. Any size penne or pasta quills will do, the larger or very small quills. The Certosa would love for you to use sausage from Siena but I submit that you need to go there in order to make that happen!

1¾	cups softened cannellini beans
1	rib celery, chopped
1	large carrot, chopped
2	bay leaves
½	medium onion
½	pound sweet Italian sausage, casing removed and meat finely chopped
½	cup white wine
1¾	cups dry penne
	Salt and pepper
	Parmesan cheese
	Italian (flat-leaf) parsley, chopped, for garnish

🌿 🌿 🌿

- Cook the beans, celery, carrot, bay leaves, and onion in just enough water to cover. Once cooked (about 15 to 20 minutes or until tender), pour two thirds of the mixture into a food processor and whirl just to purée. Set aside.
- In a skillet, quickly fry the sausage over high heat. Remove from the heat and drain any fat. Return the sausage to the pan and add the wine so that the sausage may marinate while you prepare the pasta.

- Cook the pasta in boiling salted water until *al dente.* Drain and add the macaroni to the pan with the sausage and the reserved whole beans and puréed vegetables. Add a little grated cheese and garnish with a generous helping of the chopped parsley. Serve hot.

YIELD: 4 APPETIZER SERVINGS

Castello di Spaltenna

Sherried Risotto with Green Peppercorns and Walnuts

In Italy, this dish follows the appetizer course as the pasta course. The Arborio rice takes a while to cook, but Castello di Spaltenna offers a quick way to cook short-grain rice. Instead of following the method below, use a pressure cooker. This cuts the time to prepare risotto by more than 90 percent!

¼	cup butter
1	medium onion
1	teaspoon crushed green peppercorns
½	cup coarsely chopped walnuts
1¾	cups Arborio rice
1	cup good quality cream sherry
4	cups vegetable broth
½	cup Parmesan cheese

- Heat the butter in a medium saucepan (or small pressure cooker). Add the onion and sauté until translucent. Add the peppercorns and the walnuts and let simmer for 1 to 2 minutes. Pour the rice into the pan and brown until it turns golden. Add the wine and cook over medium heat until the wine evaporates. Add the broth ½ cup at a time (or all at once, if using pressure cooker), stirring until the broth is incorporated (may take up to 25 minutes, 5 to 6 minutes in the pressure cooker). When the rice is *al dente,* (or the red tab shows up on the pressure cooker), remove the rice from the heat and stir in the Parmesan cheese. Let the rice cool for 2 to 3 minutes so that it will absorb the liquid.

YIELD: 6 SERVINGS

The penne in the Certosa di Maggiano breakfast room, where the ambience is that of a European country kitchen

La Chiusa

Risotto Primavera with Asparagus

Risotto is made throughout Italy in hundreds of different ways, despite the length of time it traditionally requires to cook the short-grain variety of rice. (See page 83 for doing risotto the quick 5-minute way in a pressure cooker.)

Another method of cooking risotto is to make it ahead of time. Cook the risotto up to the last 5 minutes and the last bit (about ½ to 1 cup) of liquid remaining. Spread the risotto out onto a baking pan

and place it, covered, in the refrigerator until close to serving time. Return it to a clean saucepan over medium-high heat. Add the liquid and cook until tender, about 5 minutes. The risotto will taste and appear as fresh as if you just made the whole thing.

2	tablespoons butter
1	large spring onion, finely chopped
1	clove garlic, minced
1	small zucchini, thinly sliced
¾	cup fresh or frozen baby peas
1	tablespoon chopped fresh basil
1	tablespoon Italian (flat-leaf) parsley, chopped
6	asparagus spears, blanched and cut into bite-size pieces
1½	cups Arborio rice
	Salt and pepper
1	small ripe tomato, peeled and diced
2	tablespoons spinach purée or thinly sliced leaves
2	tablespoons grated Parmesan cheese, or more to taste

❧ ❧ ❧

- Melt the butter in a medium saucepan over medium-high heat. Add the onion and the garlic, and sauté for 1 minute. Add the zucchini, peas, basil, parsley, and asparagus. Season with salt and pepper.
- Add enough water to just cover the rice and cook over medium-high heat, stirring. Keep adding more water, ½ cup at a time, until you use about 4 cups of water, or enough that the rice is *al dente.* Keep stirring continuously. About 5 minutes before the rice is cooked, stir in the tomatoes, spinach purée, and the Parmesan cheese. The rice is done when its texture is creamy. (Note: You may substitute a mild chicken broth for the water.)

YIELD: MAKES 2 MAIN COURSE SERVINGS OR 4 TO 6 SIDE DISHES

A classic Tuscan dish of risotto at La Chiusa

Villa Principessa Elisa

Sweet-and-Sour Prawns and Chickpeas Florentine with Tomato Concassée

The fine blending of these classic Tuscan ingredients is enhanced by the concassée, which is a typical fresh tomato pulp used prolifically in both Italian and French cuisine. You may substitute the large shrimp for prawns. The mixture of lemon juice and raspberry vinegar serves up a sweet-and-sour taste for the spinach and chickpeas.

CONCASSÉE:

2	medium tomatoes (about 1 pound)
2	tablespoons chopped fresh basil leaves

PRAWNS:

¾	cup chickpeas, soaked in water 24 hours
20	prawns or large shrimp
2	tablespoons extra virgin olive oil
1	clove garlic, minced
	Salt and pepper
	Juice of 1 lemon
1	tablespoon raspberry vinegar
12	ounces spinach, chopped into bite-size pieces

- Make the concassée. Bring a medium saucepan of water to a boil. Stem the tomatoes and score the bottoms with an X. Parboil the tomatoes in the water for 20 to 30 seconds or just until the scored edges of the skin begin to peel back. Transfer the tomatoes to a cold water bath to stop the cooking process. Once they are cool enough to handle, cut the tomatoes in half horizontally; peel off the skin and chop into a small dice. Toss in the basil leaves. Set aside.
- Add the soaked chickpeas to a medium saucepan with enough water to cover. Boil the chickpeas about 30 minutes or until tender. Drain and set aside.
- In a large bowl, mix the prawns with the olive oil and garlic. Season with salt and pepper. In a large skillet, cook the prawn mixture until the prawns turn pink and the garlic is lightly browned. Add the chickpeas and transfer to a large bowl. Set aside.
- To the same skillet, add the lemon juice and the vinegar, and sauté the spinach just until it wilts.

Wine Suggestion

The Sangiovese grape lends a delicate perfume to this light and fresh wine that is rich in fruit character. Ruffino Torgaio Sangiovese has just the right texture and refreshing taste to combine well with the sweet-and-sour flavors of this prawn dish.

Add the spinach to the chickpea mixture. Strain any excess sauce or juice and divide evenly among the serving plates. Top with a dollop of tomato concassée.

YIELD: 4 SERVINGS

The sweet-and-sour recipe in the gazebo restaurant at La Principessa Elisa in Lucca

Il Bottaccio

Salmon with Pink Pepper and Arugula

Hearty salmon is highlighted by lively pink pepper over a basis of rucola or arugula. This is low in fat and easy to prepare as an appetizer, a lunch plate, or an entrée.

Cabreo La Pietra Chardonnay,
from the **Tuscan Estates of**
Ruffino, *is a mouth-filling wine,*
with a richness of fruit that perfectly
accents the Salmon with Pink Pepper
and Arugula.

2	tablespoons olive oil
¼	cup chopped arugula, plus whole leaves for garnish
1	tablespoon ground pink pepper
	Salt
2	pounds salmon (4 filets)
½	cup fish broth for sprinkling

- Preheat the oven to 350°. Heat the oil in a heatproof casserole over low heat. Add the arugula, the pink pepper, and a little salt to taste. Turn the flame to high and cook just until the greens wilt, about 2 minutes. Place the salmon on top and sprinkle with some fish broth. Bake in the oven for about 7 minutes or until the salmon is tender. Garnish with fresh arugula and serve immediately.

YIELD: 4 SERVINGS

Il Bottaccio

Red Mullet with Fresh Beets

A fantasy of flavor and texture, red mullet is caught locally and, in this dish, only enhanced by the presence of the ruby red beets. This can be a light appetizer but very colorful and tasty. Il Bottaccio borders the Emilia-Romagna region, where half of Italy's sugar beets are produced.

2-3	small fresh beets, peeled
1	tablespoon olive oil
	Salt and freshly ground pink pepper
1½	cups fish broth
1	pound red mullet filets
	Pink peppercorns for garnish

- Cut the beets julienne style. Heat the oil in a skillet and add the beets. Add the salt and pepper and cook for 2 minutes. Add half of the fish broth and continue cooking over medium-high heat until the sauce reduces by half. Add the mullet filets, skin sides up. Season with salt and add the remaining fish broth, cooking 3 minutes more.
- Cut the filets into diagonal slices. Fan out onto individual serving plates. Garnish evenly with the beets and some whole pink peppercorns.

YIELD: 4 SERVINGS

La Chiusa

Sautéed Cod with Tomato Sauce

8	ounces dried salted cod, cut into 2-inch squares
½	cup olive oil, divided
½	medium onion, peeled and thinly sliced
1	16-ounce can peeled Italian tomatoes
	Salt and pepper
½	cup all-purpose flour

- Soak the cod in cold water for 8 hours, changing the water at least 3 times.
- When the cod has soaked, heat ¼ cup of the olive oil in a medium saucepan over medium-high heat. Add the onion and cook over

Wine Suggestion

LIBAIO

da uve *Chardonnay* e *Pinot Grigio*
di *Toscana*

RUFFINO

The richness and complex flavors of the Chardonnay grape, when married with the liveliness and fresh-fruit characteristics of Pinot Grigio, make Libaio *a perfect companion to the cod and tomato recipe.*

medium heat until lightly browned. Stir in the tomatoes, breaking them up with a spoon. Turn the heat down to a simmer and cook for about 20 minutes, seasoning with salt and pepper.

- In a separate skillet, heat the remaining olive oil over medium-high heat. Drain the cod and dust with the flour. Place the fish in the hot oil to sauté for about 2 minutes on each side. Drain on a paper towel and add the fish to the tomato sauce. Simmer for 5 minutes and serve.

YIELD: 2 SERVINGS

Villa Principessa Elisa

Sea Bass Balsamic with White Beans

Olive oil is a key ingredient in countless Italian recipes, including this sea bass. So olive trees abound in Tuscany. Lidamo Dinelli, shovel on shoulder, works this terraced olive grove at an old farm in Vorno, near Lucca.

You will need to start a day ahead of serving time to prepare this very Tuscan recipe. The white beans need to soak overnight.

1¼	cups dry white beans
1	sprig each: rosemary and thyme, plus more for garnish
1	bay leaf
3	cloves garlic, chopped
	Salt and pepper
3	tablespoons olive oil, divided, plus more for drizzling
¾	cup fish stock
1	pound sea bass filets, cut diagonally into ¼-inch thick slices
¼	cup balsamic vinegar

- Soak the beans in cold water for 24 hours. Next day, cook the soaked beans over medium-low heat, begining in cold water to cover, with the rosemary, thyme, and the bay leaf. Add I of the cloves of garlic, and salt and pepper to taste. Cook the beans and seasonings for 30 to 40 minutes, or until tender.
- When the beans are cooked, heat a large skillet with I tablespoon of the olive oil. Sauté the remaining garlic in the oil until lightly browned. Add the fish stock and cook about 10 minutes more. Stir in the vinegar and cook for about 2 minutes more. Remove from the heat and keep warm. Remove and discard the herb sprigs and bay leaf.
- Heat I tablespoon of the olive oil in a large skillet. Add the fish to the heated skillet and cook quickly, just until the fish is tender. Turn the fish and continue to cook until lightly browned.
- To assemble the dish, evenly divide the fish and add the bean mixture. Drizzle the beans with a flourish of remaining olive oil.

YIELD: 4 SERVINGS

These four Italian soldiers are just as happy as any other tourists to be visiting Siena on a sunny day in spring.

🌿 🌿 🌿

- Remove the filets from the chicken and place the filets in a blender with the artichokes, egg yolk, and cream. Add a little salt and pepper. Blend just to obtain a thick liquid.
- Make a cut halfway into each chicken breast. Fill the pocket with the artichoke purée.
- Heat about 2 tablespoons olive oil in a nonstick skillet. Fry the stuffed chicken in the pan until browned. Add the white wine to deglaze the pan. Add the stock and the flour, and cook over medium heat for 15 to 20 minutes. Remove from the pan and cut each breast into slices (about ½-inch thick.) Fan out onto 2 individual serving plates and pour the sauce from the pan on top.

YIELD: 2 SERVINGS

Certosa di Maggiano

Chicken Breast Stuffed with Artichoke Purée

"Impressive" is one way to describe this entrée. "Full of flavor and interest" is another. No matter how you slice these chicken breasts, they look impressive and taste great.

2	boneless, skinless chicken breasts, with filets, pounded thin
2	artichoke hearts, cut into slices and sautéed in olive oil
1	egg yolk
2	tablespoons heavy cream
	Salt and pepper
2	tablespoons olive oil
1	cup white wine
1	cup chicken stock or broth
	All-purpose flour

*W*ine Suggestion

The medium-bodied Aziano Chianti Classico displays a luscious fruit character that makes it a perfect partner with the pronounced flavors in the Chicken Breast Stuffed with Artichoke Purée.

Certosa di Maggiano

Roasted Fowl with Cheese Fondue

Pecorino cheese, from sheep's milk is made all over Italy. But the Pecorino produced in Tuscany is said to be the best. Any imported Pecorino will work in this recipe. Guinea fowl is available in most parts of the United States—at least in frozen form, if not fresh. This recipe will work with any game poultry such as chicken or partridge. Feel free to substitute for the guinea fowl, which is typical of Tuscany, but not, perhaps, of your neighborhood market.

1	medium guinea fowl, cleaned (giblets removed) (about 2½ pounds)
	Salt and pepper
2	cloves garlic
1	sprig fresh rosemary
2	tablespoons olive oil or more for frying
½	cup red wine

SAUCE:

¼	cup (½ stick) butter
½	cup all-purpose flour
4	cups chicken stock
1½	cups coarsely chopped Pecorino cheese
	Salt and pepper

- Preheat the oven to 350°. Salt and pepper the outside and inside of the bird. Place the garlic and rosemary inside the cavity. In a large pan, heat the olive oil and fry the hen until browned on all sides. Place the hen in an ovenproof glass baking dish and pour the red wine over it. Place

A flamboyant parade complete with medieval costumes provides the kind of excitement you can expect from a visit to Florence.

in the oven and roast for 35 to 40 minutes or until tender. Baste regularly with the red wine.

- Prepare the cheese sauce while the hen roasts. Melt the butter in a large saucepan and stir in the flour, mixing well. When the flour is incorporated, pour in the stock and beat vigorously with a wire whisk to avoid lumps. Cook over medium-high heat, stirring often, for about 10 minutes. Add the cheese and transfer all to a double boiler, cooking until the cheese melts. Stir well.

- Cut the fowl into 4 quarters and serve topped with the cheese sauce.

YIELD: 4 SERVINGS

La Chiusa

Rabbit with Garlic in a Rosemary-and-Sage Tomato Sauce

Rabbit is said to be leaner even than chicken and its taste and texture are, to me, also superior. A gentle touch of fresh lemon, the soothing scents of rosemary and sage, and this dish can only be described as mouth-watering.

1	pound rabbit filets (4 filets)
6	sprigs fresh rosemary
6	fresh sage leaves
5	cloves garlic, thinly sliced
¼	cup olive oil
	Zest from 1 lemon
1	carrot, peeled and thinly sliced
8	ounces whole canned tomatoes, with liquid

- Place the filets in a baking dish and sprinkle generously with fresh rosemary leaves from 2 sprigs. Add 3 sage leaves, 4 cloves of the garlic and the oil, and marinate for 8 hours, turning occasionally.
- When ready to cook the rabbit, heat a medium saucepan over high heat and add the rabbit, with the marinade, and the lemon zest. Sauté the rabbit until browned on all sides. Turn the heat down to a simmer and add the carrot and the remaining sage and garlic. Simmer for 15 minutes. Add the tomatoes and cook on low for another 15 minutes.
- Remove the rabbit from the saucepan, turn the heat up to high and allow the sauce to reduce by half, about 10 minutes. Meanwhile, slice the rabbit into ¼-inch thick pieces. Spoon the slices and the sauce onto a serving plate. Garnish with the remaining rosemary sprigs.

YIELD: 4 SERVINGS

Wine Suggestion

The rabbit dish deserves an elegant, robust wine such as Riserva Ducale (The Duke's Reserve) from the Tuscan Estates of Ruffino. The Sangiovese grape provides a concentration of fruit and excellent structure for a truly classic pairing.

La Chiusa

Baked Tuscan Duck Breast with Fennel Sauce

As Italian immigrants, we always called fennel *finocchio* (we pronounced it fin-oy-ck). It was served mainly as a palate cleanser between courses. Indeed, today, I still do that at my house. This fragrant, graceful green resembles anise in flavor, and when cooked, takes on an even lighter, more elusive taste. Here, it is a superb complement to the gamey taste of the duck. The recipe calls for using the fresh fennel as well as fennel seeds.

You may wish to substitute duck breast for the whole duck, in which case you need about 1½ pounds of duck breast.

1	whole duck (about 2½ pounds)
	Salt and pepper
1	cup (2 sticks) butter, cut into pats
2	tablespoons fennel seeds, crushed
	Fennel greens and ribs for garnish

- Preheat the oven to 350°. Salt and pepper the duck. Rub the butter into the duck, covering the entire bird. Sprinkle generously with the crushed fennel seeds. Place in a baking dish.

- Bake the duck for 45 minutes to 1 hour or until brown and crispy. Transfer the duck to a cutting board and when the duck is cool enough to handle, cut out the breast meat and then slice thinly across the grain. Place the meat onto a serving platter.

- Place the baking pan with its juices (or transfer to a sauté pan) on the stovetop and cook over high heat until the liquid is reduced by half. Pour the juices over the sliced duck and garnish with fennel greens and bulbs.

YIELD: 2 SERVINGS

Wine Suggestion

TENUTA
SANTEDAME

CHIANTI CLASSICO

DENOMINAZIONE DI ORIGINE CONTROLLATA E GARANTITA

BOTTLED BY CHIANTI RUFFINO
SpA · PONTASSIEVE · ITALIA · 326/FI
PRODUCT OF ITALY

TENIMENTI
RUFFINO

750 ml e   ALC. 12.5% BY VOL.

A single-vineyard Chianti Classico with deep fruit flavor and hearty structure, Santedame from the Tuscan Estates of Ruffino is the perfect accompaniment to baked duck as well as to pork, veal, chicken, and red meats.

Locanda dell' Amorosa

Beef Medallions with Potato Cakes and Lettuce Sauce

Although this is primarily a dinner entrée, you can also make this for a special lunch. The lettuce sauce is tangy and tasty and a nice catalyst for bringing out the flavor of the beef.

BEEF:

2	pounds beef loin
	Salt and pepper
¼	cup extra virgin olive oil, divided

POTATO CAKES:

3	pounds white potatoes
	Vegetable oil for frying

SAUCE:

1	cup fresh lettuce (of choice)
¼	cup fresh chives
¼	cup fresh basil leaves
2	tablespoons balsamic vinegar

- Cut the loin into medallions of about 8 to 10 ounces each. Season them with salt and pepper. In a large skillet, heat 1 tablespoon of the olive oil and sauté the meat over high heat until lightly browned, about 5 minutes per side. Grate the potatoes and season them with salt and pepper. Form the potatoes into cakes and place them in a frying pan of hot oil to cover. Cook until the potato cakes turn a golden brown. Drain on a paper towel and set aside.
- In a blender or food processor, whirl together the lettuce, the remaining olive oil, the chives, basil, and the vinegar, and add a sprinkling of salt and pepper to taste. Blend for about 5 minutes until smooth.
- To serve, place a medallion of beef on top of a potato cake. Drape with the lettuce sauce and serve.

YIELD: 4 SERVINGS

Castello di Spaltenna

Medallions of Roasted Veal Shank with a Vegetable Wine Sauce

The shank portion of the calf is very tough but full of flavor. Because of its toughness, the meat needs to cook for a long time until it almost shreds off the bone. The vegetables serve to make a nice base for a sauce. After baking, deglaze the pan with red wine.

1	red onion, peeled and sliced
3	ribs celery, sliced
3	carrots, peeled and sliced
2	leeks (top and bottom), cleaned and coarsely chopped
4	spring onions, sliced
4	pounds veal shank
	Salt and pepper
¾	cup olive oil, divided
3	cups white wine
½	cup or more beef broth
1	cup red wine

- Preheat the oven to 400°. Place the onion, celery, carrots, leek, and spring onions in the bottom of a large roasting pan. Rub the veal well with salt and pepper and add to pan. Pour ½ cup of the olive oil into the pan along with the white wine.
- Bake for 30 to 45 minutes or until the veal is browned. Lower the temperature to 325°. Bake 1 hour and 30 minutes more, or until the veal is very tender or reaches an internal temperature of 170°. If the veal becomes too brown, cover with aluminum foil to finish the cooking. Meanwhile, watch the vegetables and add broth at intervals, just to keep the onions from caramelizing.
- To carve, slice or shred chunks of meat lengthwise from the bone. Drizzle with the remaining olive oil. Deglaze the pan with the red wine and spoon this liquid over the meat to serve.

YIELD: 6 SERVINGS

Il Bottaccio

Wild Boar Steak with Berry Sauce

The rugged terrain of the woods of Tuscany produces the wild boar for this dish. The robust flavor of the steak is paired with wine and fruits of the forest. The sweetness of the berries and wine complement the smoldering wilderness of the meat already marinated and redolent with memorable spices. You will need to start this dish a day ahead of serving time. If you cannot find wild boar, substitute almost any gamey meat.

MARINADE:

4	cups light red wine (not dry)
1	tablespoon juniper berries (or substitute dried cranberries)
5	whole cloves
1	tablespoon coriander seed

STEAKS:

3	tablespoons olive oil
½	cup blackberries, strawberries, and/or raspberries
4	wild boar steaks (about ½ pound each)
	Salt and freshly ground white pepper
½	cup rosé wine
½	cup crème de cassis or raspberry liqueur
1	cup vegetable broth
	Fresh berries for garnish

- Marinate the steaks in the wine and spices for 24 hours in the refrigerator. Next day, heat the oil in a skillet. Crush the berries slightly and add them to the oil. Add the steaks and the salt and pepper to taste.
- Add the rosé and cook over medium heat until the alcohol evaporates, about 3 minutes. Remove the steaks from the pan and set aside. Add the cassis and vegetable broth and cook, reducing the liquid by a third. Return the steaks to the pan and cook for another 2 minutes. Serve the steaks basted in the juice and add fresh berries for garnish.

YIELD: 4 SERVINGS

Il Bottaccio

Provolone-Stuffed Veal Roll in a Wine-Cream Sauce

¼	**cup olive oil, divided**
2	**cups thinly sliced radicchio lettuce**
	Salt and pepper
12	**ounces veal steak, cut ½-inch thick**
4	**ounces Provolone cheese**
⅓	**cup port wine**
¼	**cup red wine**
¼	**cup heavy cream**

* Preheat the oven to 400°. Heat the olive oil in a small skillet over medium-high heat. Add the radicchio, seasoning it with salt and pepper. Sauté the lettuce for about 2 minutes, just until it wilts.
* Using a meat mallet, pound the veal to ½-inch thickness. Season both sides with salt and pepper.
* Lay the cheese slices on top of the veal. Remove the lettuce from the pan and arrange atop the cheese. Roll the veal up and secure with tooth-picks. Cut the veal roll in half to form 2 rolls. Add the remaining olive oil to an ovenproof skillet and heat over medium-high heat. When hot, add the veal rolls and cook until browned on all sides.
* Add the port and the red wine and bake the veal roll in the oven for 15 minutes until the wine has reduced by half. Return the pan to medium heat on the stovetop and add the cream. Stir well to incorporate. Cook a few minutes to reduce by half.

* Remove the pan from the heat. Place the veal on a cutting board. Remove the toothpicks and cut the veal into ½-inch-thick slices. Drizzle the sauce over the veal.

YIELD: 4 SERVINGS

The stuffed veal roll at Il Bottaccio

Longtime La Chiusa gardener Novilio Marcocci picks poppies for the restaurant in the Tuscan village of Montefollonico.

Locanda dell' Amorosa

Baked Caramel Apple Crisp

2	pounds Granny Smith apples or other tart cooking apples
¼	cup plus 1 tablespoon butter
¾	cup sugar

PASTRY:

1	cup all-purpose flour
2	eggs
3	tablespoons butter
¼	cup sugar

- Preheat the oven to 450°. Peel, core, and cut the apples into ½-inch slices. In a heavily greased 9-inch cake pan or iron skillet melt the butter and the sugar over moderate heat.

- As soon as the butter and sugar start to caramelize, place the apples into the mixture, stirring the fruit in carefully with a wooden spoon. Stir until the apples are well coated with the caramel. Place the apples into the oven and bake for about 10 minutes until the sauce starts to bubble. Remove the apples from the oven and let cool.

- While the apples bake, prepare the crust. Mix together the flour, eggs, butter, and sugar to form a dough. Roll the dough out large enough to cover the cake pan, about ½-inch thickness or less. Cover the cake pan with the pastry, sealing it well without any air inside. (Do not allow the crust to fall over the outside of the pan.) Return the pan to the oven and bake for 30 minutes or until the crust is golden brown.

- Remove the cake from the oven and turn it out onto a platter. Serve warm.

YIELD: 6 SERVINGS

La Chiusa

Pear Sorbet

	Juice of 2 lemons
4	pears, peeled and cored
1	cup water
¼	cup sugar
2	tablespoons Pear William liqueur
	Fresh mint for garnish

- Pour the lemon juice over the peeled pears to prevent browning. In a small saucepan, make a simple or sugar syrup by bringing to a boil the water and sugar. Cook over gentle heat until thick and syrupy, about 20 to 30 minutes.
- Prepare the pears by bringing a medium saucepan of water to a gentle boil and add the pears with their lemon juice (making sure the water covers the pears). Poach the pears in the lemony water for about 10 minutes until they are very tender. Drain the pears and place them in a food processor, puréing them until thick.
- Mix in the Pear William and ½ cup of the syrup (reserving the rest of the syrup for another recipe). Pour the mixture into a stainless steel container and freeze. Cover after the sorbet has solidified.
- To serve, scoop the sorbet into goblets and garnish with mint.

YIELD: 4 SERVINGS

Certosa di Maggiano

Tuscan Bread Pudding with Mascarpone-and-Almond Sauce

Mascarpone cheese is a buttery cheese made from cow's milk, used frequently in Italian desserts. It is available in supermarkets and specialty food stores. Begin this recipe the night before serving. This bread pudding, with the Italian twist of cheese and almonds, is irresistible.

PUDDING:

2¼	cups or more thinly sliced crusty Italian bread
2	cups whole milk
3	egg yolks
¾	cup sugar
½	cup sultanas or dark raisins
½	cup strawberry or any flavored jam
½	cup honey

SAUCE:

3	egg yolks
¾	cup sugar
1½	cups Mascarpone cheese
½	cup chopped almonds

- Soak the bread in the milk overnight. Next morning, preheat the oven to 350°. Add the remaining pudding ingredients to the bread, stirring with a wooden spoon until mixed well. Butter a 9x13-inch baking dish, pour in the pudding, and bake in a bain-marie in the oven for 40 minutes or until a tester inserted comes clean.

- While the pudding bakes, prepare the sauce. Whip the egg yolks with the sugar until incorporated. Mix in the Mascarpone, being careful to mix from underneath upwards to avoid causing the cream to settle. Fold in the almonds and serve over the pudding.

YIELD: 6 SERVINGS

Certosa di Maggiano

Pine-Nut-and-Raisin Pie

For something different and very Tuscan, try this *pignolata* or simple pine-nut pie, made with 2 crusts, a layer of cream, raisins, and pignoli nuts.

CRUST:

1½	cups (3 sticks) butter
1	cup sugar
3	egg yolks
2	cups all-purpose flour
⅛	teaspoon salt
1	teaspoon grated orange peel

CREAM:

4	cups whole milk
	Peel of ½ lemon
8	egg yolks
1	cup sugar
½	cup all-purpose flour
¼	cup raisins
¼	cup pine nuts or pignoli

Monilla Marcacci, Maria Mari, and Tonnini Tosca (l to r)—knitting while the sun shines brightly on the Piazza Grande of Montepulciano

- In a large bowl, mix together the butter and sugar until well incorporated. Mix in the egg yolks, one at a time. Add the flour, salt, and orange peel, and mix just until combined (do not overmix) and the dough holds together. Allow the dough to rest in the refrigerator for about 20 minutes.
- Meanwhile, prepare the cream filling. In a large nonstick saucepan, bring the milk and lemon peel to a boil. Remove from the heat immediately and let cool down to warm. Beat in egg yolks, sugar, and flour. Return saucepan to medium heat and simmer for 10 minutes. Stir in the raisins.
- Preheat the oven to 350°. Remove the dough from the refrigerator. Divide the dough in half. Roll out each piece of the dough to ¼-inch thickness. Fit one piece of the dough into a 9x13-inch baking dish. Pour in the cream mixture and fit the other rolled piece of dough over it. Brush the surface with whisked egg and sprinkle with the pignoli. Bake 35 to 40 minutes or until tester inserted comes out clean.

YIELD: 8 SERVINGS

Villa Principessa Elisa

Vanilla Gelato with Strawberry-Caramel Sauce

Gelato or *gelati* means ice cream in Italian. Gelaterias are ice cream parlors, found all over Italy, even in the more remote countryside towns such as Siena, from where this recipe hails. Chef Antonio Sanna offers up a splendidly refreshing treat with his native frozen dessert that is much creamier and denser in taste and texture than American ice cream, primarily because it is made with a lot less air.

GELATO:

2½	cups milk, divided
⅛	teaspoon salt
1	vanilla bean
¾	cup sugar
5	egg yolks
1	egg white, whipped to a froth with a pinch of salt

CARAMEL SAUCE:

1	cup sugar
¼	cup water
½	pint strawberries

Sunset view of Siena and the Certosa di Maggiano bell tower (right)—from the olive grove on the grounds of the former monastery

ASSEMBLY:

	Fresh mint
4	**whole strawberries**

The Tuscan hill town of Montepulciano rises above the morning mist—as seen from the grounds of La Chiusa's restaurant.

- Make the ice cream far enough in advance to allow 2 to 3 hours to freeze. In a medium saucepan, heat all but ¼ cup of the milk, adding the salt, the vanilla bean, and the sugar. Remove the mixture from the heat and discard the bean.
- Meanwhile, in a mixing bowl, beat the egg yolks, then slowly add in the reserved cold milk. Then slowly add the hot milk, stirring constantly. When the ingredients are well blended, transfer back into the saucepan and heat for about 2 minutes, stirring.
- Pour the mixture into a bowl and let cool, stirring occasionally. Pour the mixture through a fine sieve into a container, adding the frothy egg white halfway through the process. (The egg white helps make the ice cream smooth and soft.) Freeze.
- To prepare the caramel sauce, place the sugar in a small saucepan over medium-high heat. As the sugar begins to dissolve and reaches a syrupy consistency, remove the mixture from the heat and add the water, just to thin the syrup. (Add the water gradually, as you do not want the syrup to be runny.) Cook the mixture over a low flame until it turns a golden brown, a few min-utes. Keep stirring constantly to prevent sticking and burning. Remove from the heat. Hull and slice the strawberries and add them to the syrup.
- To service, place a scoop of ice cream in the center of each plate and pour the sauce evenly among 4 individual dishes. Garnish with a sprig of mint and a whole strawberry.

YIELD: 4 SERVINGS

France is a country where you can still find that most civilized amenity, the restaurant table for one. With nothing as frivolous as conversation to distract him, the gourmet can give his full attention to the plate and the glass, lifting his head occasionally between mouthfuls to nod for a second bottle or another basket of bread, acknowledging nobody except the waiter, at peace with his stomach. At last, with maybe a digestif and a muffled belch to help him on his way, he pushes back his chair and leaves, stopping only to ask what's for lunch tomorrow.

Peter Mayle (with M. Loxton), *Provence*

FRANCE

ÎLE DE FRANCE

❧ ❧ ❧

The Pot-au-Feu and Paris' Joie de Vivre

The so-called City of Lights, having reached the ultimate in cosmopolitan flavor, is nonetheless still aglow with the excitement of food and an irrepressible spirit for life or joie de vivre.

Everywhere you look, the sidewalks are bustling with shoppers, sightseers, and the business crowd. And you have to ask, "What's really most important here?" And the answer—as you look around at the cafe awnings, the white-tablecloth bistros, the petite brasseries, the colorful patisseries, the dependable boulangeries, and the traditional charcuteries—is, of course, the food.

Although the city has certainly become more homogenized over the years, Paris still has a way with local specialties. Baguettes are typically Parisian and can be found in the bakeries or boulangeries all over the city. Breads are baked twice a day, so bakery windows are also well-stocked with breads standing sentinel until the end of the day, when everyone has gone home to enjoy the crusty loaves with French wines and local cheeses.

Dining on a terrace at Le Marignan-Elysées provides an Eiffel Tower view to accompany the Prawn Salad with Arugula and Lemon-Mustard Dressing, the Chocolate Policeman's Hat (recipes on pages 108 and 116), and a dish of greens.

Paris is a haven for cheese lovers, with some of the best Brie being made just outside of the city in the Île de France region. A fromage blanc or fresh cream cheese usually ends the meal with or without cream and sugar.

The pork stores, with their myriad styles of sausage links hanging from strings, now have counters where you can order a fast meal. They are a good way to sample Paris' vestiges of regional cuisine. Many Parisians take the charcuterie for granted but visitors are wise enough to take out a pork lunch—maybe a pâté and a baguette—and find a quiet spot in one of the region's charming parks.

Parisians are particularly fond of their pot-au-feu, a boiled meat stew that is made with a variety of beef and vegetables with special sauces. The pot-au-feu is a one-dish meal, often cooked in a copper or pottery dish with a tight-fitting lid so it can simmer slowly.

Beers are also heralded in this region and considered some of the best anywhere. Beer is often chosen first and then a meal is designed around the particular brew, depending on its characteristics.

The Île de France region is a gourmet's paradise, where the creativity of chefs is accepted and applauded. Supporting all of this love of food, Paris' markets are spectacular, overflowing with the freshest ingredients from all over France. It is not hard to see why Paris is still the market basket for France and a good area to look to for French recipes to try in the home kitchen.

hand. Dust with flour and shape into small ovals. Place them on a parchment-lined baking tray. Allow the rolls to rise at room temperature for three to four hours.
- Preheat the oven to 450° and bake the loaves for about 15 minutes or until golden brown.

YIELD: 12 ROLLS

Le Marignan-Elysées

Baked-Olive Mini-Loaves

With a touch of the Provençal, this bread may accompany dinner as well as lunch with a splendid salad. To reheat these mini-loaves, sprinkle them lightly with water and heat, covered, in a 400° oven.

2¼	cups all-purpose flour, plus more for dusting
1	teaspoon yeast
1	teaspoon olive oil
¼	tablespoon salt
½	cup water
½	cup pitted green olives
½	cup pitted black olives

- Place all of the ingredients, except the olives, in a bowl of an electric mixer. Mix for 5 minutes until a dough is formed. Stop the beater and add the olives. Complete the kneading at a lower speed. Remove the dough from the bowl and let rest for 15 to 30 minutes in a warm place or until risen and double in size.
- With a knife, cut up the dough evenly, dividing it into little balls, using about ¼ cup dough for each. Roll these out with the palm of your

Le Parc Victor Hugo

Satiny Pumpkin Soup

Pumpkin soup is always a favorite. Remember to freeze your own pumpkin meat in the fall so that you may prepare this dish any time of year. See the interesting pumpkin soup variation including coconut and saffron on page 153.

2	pounds fresh pumpkin, cubed
1	quart chicken stock
2	teaspoons sugar
2	tablespoons cornstarch
3	tablespoons water
1¼	cups heavy cream
6	tablespoons unsalted butter, chilled and cut into pieces
	Sea salt and freshly ground white pepper

- In a medium stockpot, combine the pumpkin, chicken stock, and sugar. Cover and bring the mixture to a boil. Turn the mixture down to a simmer and cook for about 18 minutes. (Pumpkin should cook quickly to avoid bitterness.) Once the pumpkin has cooked, transfer the mixture to a food processor and purée until smooth.

- Strain through a coarse sieve and return the puréed pumpkin to the stockpot over high heat.
- In a small bowl, dissolve the cornstarch in the water.
- When the pumpkin returns to a boil, skim off any scum that may arise. Remove the pot from the heat and quickly whisk in the cornstarch. Stir in the cream and bring the mixture back to a boil. Purée the mixture again in the food processor, this time incorporating the butter. The soup should have a velvety, creamy consistency.
- Return the soup to the stockpot over moderate heat and season with salt and pepper. (Do not salt the soup during cooking, for the chicken stock should season the soup sufficiently during the cooking process.) Serve immediately.

YIELD: 6 TO 8 SERVINGS

The Satiny Pumpkin Soup (left) in the courtyard at Le Parc Victor Hugo

Le Marignan-Elysées

Prawn Salad with Arugula and Lemon-Mustard Dressing

This easy salad is served at Marignan as an appetizer, but you may also serve this refreshing and tasty dish as a luncheon plate. It would go well with the olive loaves on page 106.

VINAIGRETTE DRESSING:

¼	cup lemon juice
¾	cup olive oil
1	teaspoon coarse-grained mustard
	Salt and pepper

PRAWNS:

36	prawns, cleaned and deveined
1	bunch arugula
1	clove garlic
	Salt and pepper

- Whisk together the ingredients for the vinaigrette dressing, adding the salt and pepper to taste.
- Boil the shrimp just until they turn pink. Remove from the water and let cool in the refrigerator.
- Clean the arugula, removing the stalks. Season the arugula with salt and pepper. Cut the garlic into slivers.
- To present the dish, place the arugula onto 6 individual serving plates. Place 6 shrimp on the arugula. Evenly divide the dressing among the six plates. Add a few garlic slivers. Season with salt and pepper.

YIELD: 6 SERVINGS

Domaine Chandon Réserve *has the rich, toasted flavors, elegant complex fruit, and fine beads (bubbles) that characterize the best sparkling wines.*

Le Marignan-Elysées

Pan-Fried Red Mullet with Tapenade

Tapenade is an olive paste that originated in Provence. It is used alone with bread and crackers or included in many recipes right in the cooking process. Here, it serves as a coating for fried mullet. Mullet may be purchased in red or gray varieties. Any mullet will do. Have your fishmonger prepare the fish into filets, bones removed.

FISH:

6	mullet filets (6 or 8 ounces each)
¼	cup olive oil

Pan-Fried Red Mullet with Tapenade in the casual Le Table du Marche Restaurant at Le Marignan-Elysées, where baskets of Baked-Olive Mini-Loaves (recipe on page 106) are found on every table

speed until the mixture forms a paste. Transfer the mixture to a small bowl and set aside.

- Cut the zucchini (skins included) into balls, using a melon baller. Heat 1 tablespoon of the olive oil in a medium skillet and add the zucchini balls. Season with salt and sauté until *al dente.*
- Slice the potatoes into ¼-inch rounds. In another skillet, heat the remaining 2 tablespoons of olive oil. Fry the rounds in the oil until crisp.
- Place the mullet in a frying pan and cook the fish until browned, about 1 minute per side. Remove the pan from the heat.
- Assemble the dish by setting out 6 individual serving plates. Arrange the potatoes onto each plate as a bed. Add a fish filet to each dish. Spread tapenade over each piece of fish. Add the zucchini balls and a trickle of olive oil.

YIELD: 6 SERVINGS

Olives are used prolifically in French cooking—as in this seafood recipe.

TAPENADE:

1	cup pitted black olives
2	anchovy filets
2	fresh basil leaves
1	teaspoon capers
1½	teaspoons sherry wine vinegar
	Salt and pepper

ASSEMBLY:

3	small zucchini
3	tablespoons olive oil, plus more for drizzling
12	small white potatoes, unpeeled, boiled until tender

- Brush the filets with the olive oil and place in the refrigerator.
- Prepare the tapenade. Place all of the tapenade ingredients into a food processor, seasoning with salt and pepper to taste. Blend at high

Baked Tomato Tartlets with Garden Vegetables

Sautéed tomatoes and a garden variety of vegetables team up with a flaky pastry to crown your appetizer plate. This recipe is simple and delicious.

PASTRY:

¾	cup all-purpose flour
¼	cup water
½	teaspoon or less salt

TOMATO FILLING:

¾	pound red ripe tomatoes, blanched and peeled
	Salt and pepper
¼	cup olive oil
1	shallot

VEGETABLES:

1	bunch asparagus
1¼	cups fresh young peas
3	small artichokes

ASSEMBLY:

8	ounces fresh anchovy filets
4	ounces arugula
¼	cup pitted black olives
	Juice of 1 lemon
½	cup olive oil

- Prepare the pastry in a mixing bowl, combining the flour, water, and salt. Form a dough and knead until smooth and elastic. Let rest at room temperature for 1 hour or until doubled in size. Then roll the dough out with a rolling pin to about ¼-inch thickness. Cut the pastry up into small pieces, about 4 to 5 inches each, to form the crust for 6 tartlets. Set aside.
- Slice the tomatoes in half and press each half with your hand to remove the liquid and seeds. Coarsely chop the tomatoes and season with salt and pepper.
- In a medium saucepan, heat the ¼ cup of olive oil and sauté the shallot. Add the chopped tomato and the garlic and cook over low heat for 30 minutes, or until all of the liquid has evaporated. Remove the garlic cloves and season with salt and pepper to taste. Set aside to cool.
- Peel the asparagus and snap off the woody ends. Cook until tender in water or steam. Set aside to cool.
- Shell the peas and cook in salted water. Drain and let cool.

- Remove the leaves of the artichokes, then remove the heart and cut each one into six even slices. Set aside.
- Spear the anchovy filets with toothpicks.
- Preheat the oven to 450°. Roll out pastry into disks. Spread the tomato filling onto the pastry disks and bake the tartlets for 6 to 7 minutes or until the crusts turn golden.
- Meanwhile, heat the ½ cup of olive oil in a skillet and sauté the asparagus, peas, and artichoke hearts. Lightly coat the anchovies with olive oil and grill for 30 seconds.
- To serve, spread arugula onto individual serving plates. Arrange the tartlets on top and add the sautéd vegetables, followed by an anchovy and an olive or two. Sprinkle with some olive oil and lemon juice.

YIELD: 6 SERVINGS

Le Grand Vefour

Salmon and Eggplant Terrine

TERRINE:

3	gelatin leaves or ¼ ounce gelatin
4	small eggplants
1	salmon filet (about 2 pounds)
	Salt and pepper
¼	cup chopped fresh parsley

ASSEMBLY:

2	tablespoons poppy seeds
	Extra virgin olive oil

- Preheat the oven to 350°. Soak the gelatin leaves in 1 cup of water.
- Prick the eggplant skins and roast the eggplant in the oven for about 20 minutes or until tender. Remove the eggplants from the oven and peel away the skin, discarding it. Purée the pulp until uniformly thick. You will need about 1 cup of eggplant purée. Add the softened gelatin leaves to the eggplant purée, incorporating the leaves so that they dissolve into the eggplant.
- Divide the salmon filet into 3 equal lengths, making sure there are no bones. Season the salmon with salt and pepper on both sides. Place the salmon under a broiler and roast for a few minutes, just enough to heat the salmon through (you do not want it to brown in any way).
- Using a terrine mold pan (or substitute with a loaf pan), place a layer of the eggplant purée along the bottom. Add some chopped parsley and a piece of the salmon. Repeat again, using up all of the salmon and eggplant. Place in the refrigerator covered with plastic for 12 hours.
- To serve, cut 2 slices of the terrine and place the slices onto an individual serving plate. Brush with a little bit of olive oil and decorate with the poppy seeds. Serve with a dollop of crème fraîche (see page 186), if desired.

YIELD: 8 SERVINGS

Old-Fashioned Veal-and-Vegetable Stew

"Delicate, fragrant, flavorful, with an abundance of colorful vegetables," is how this stew, also called a *blanquette de veau* or blanket of veal, is described in Chef Joel Robuchon's cookbook *Simply French*. The book is the official cookbook of Le Parc Hotel's Relais du Parc restaurant.

1	pound veal shoulder, cut into 1-inch cubes
1	pound veal breast, cut into 1-inch cubes
2	tablespoons coarse sea salt
6	whole white peppercorns
1	medium onion
1	carrot, finely chopped
1	leek, white part only
2	ribs celery
2	large garlic cloves, cut in half
1	bouquet garni of several parsley stems, celery leaves, and sprigs of thyme, wrapped in the green part of a leek and securely fastened with cotton twine.

GARNISH:

8	spring onions, white part only
4	small inner ribs of celery
12	thin asparagus spears, woody ends snapped
12	(young) baby carrots
12	(young) baby turnips
1	small fennel bulb, coarsely chopped
3	ounces (young) tender green beans
7	ounces baby onions (or substitute pearl onions)
1	tablespoon sugar
7	ounces horn-of-plenty (chanterelle) or other wild mushrooms
7	ounces domestic (button or other) mushrooms, trimmed
3	tablespoons unsalted butter
2	tablespoons freshly squeezed lemon juice
¾	cup crème fraîche (see pages 186)
3	egg yolks
	Freshly grated nutmeg

- Place the veal in a large stockpot. Add cold water to cover and 1 tablespoon of the salt. Bring the water to a boil over high heat. Boil for 2 minutes. Remove the meat with a slotted spoon and rinse the meat quickly under the cold running water. Discard the cooking liquid. Return the meat to a large clean saucepan, add cold water to cover, and season with the remaining salt and the peppercorns. Bring the water to a boil over high heat. With a slotted spoon, regularly skim the foam that rises to the surface. When the foam subsides, add the onion, carrot, leek, celery, garlic, and the bouquet garni. Turn the heat down to a simmer. Cover the pan and cook for 2 hours.

- Meanwhile, prepare the vegetable garnish. Using kitchen twine, individually tie into bundles the leeks, celery, and asparagus. Place the leek and celery bundles into a large stockpot, along with the carrots, turnips, and fennel. Add cold water to cover and bring to a boil over high heat. When the water boils, season with salt. Prepare a large bowl of ice water. With a slotted spoon, remove each vegetable as soon as it is cooked. Transfer the vegetables to the ice water to set the color and stop the cooking process. Drain the vegetables and set them aside. (Cooking times will vary with each vegetable according to size. The vegetables should be just cooked through, still crisp and tender.)

- Prepare a large bowl of ice water for the green beans and asparagus. Set aside. Bring a large pot of water to a boil over high heat. Salt the water and add the green beans. Cook until crisp tender, about 4 minutes. Remove the beans with a slotted spoon and place in the ice water. Drain the beans and set them aside. In the same boiling water, cook the asparagus until tender, about 4 minutes. Remove with a slotted spoon and place in the ice water. Drain and set aside.

- In a medium skillet, combine the baby onions with the sugar and a taste of salt. Add water to cover by half and cook over moderately low heat until most of the water has evaporated and the onions are soft and slightly golden, but not browned. Remove the skillet from the heat and set aside.

- Place the mushrooms in a medium skillet and salt to taste. Cover the pan and cook the mushrooms over moderate heat for 3 to 4 minutes. Drain off the liquid and set the mushrooms aside until cool enough to handle. With your hands, squeeze the mushrooms over the sink to extract any remaining liquid. Set aside.

- In the same skillet, combine the domestic mushrooms (if they are very large, quarter them first) and 1 tablespoon of the unsalted butter, and all of the lemon juice. Cover and cook over moderate heat until tender, about 5 minutes. Transfer the mushrooms to a bowl and set aside. Add the mushroom cooking liquid to the simmering meat mixture.

- When the meat has cooked, transfer it to a large, clean saucepan. Add the mushrooms and onions. Cover and set aside.

- Place a piece of moistened cheesecloth over a large mesh sieve, set over a large clean saucepan. Strain the veal cooking liquid, discarding the vegetables cooked with the veal. Increase the heat to high and reduce the veal broth by half, about 5 minutes. Meanwhile, in a large bowl, combine 1 tablespoon of the crème fraîche, the egg yolks, and the nutmeg, and stir to blend. Set aside.

- Once the broth has reduced by half, whisk in the remaining crème fraîche. Return the mixture to a boil, and reduce by a third (about 3 to 4 minutes). Transfer a ladleful of the broth to the egg-yolk mixture and whisk thoroughly. Continue whisking, adding another ladleful of broth. Slowly pour the egg-yolk mixture into the broth. Reduce the heat and cook for 5 minutes, stirring occasionally to prevent the egg yolks from coagulating. (Do not let the mixture boil.) The sauce will thicken ever so slightly.

- Strain the sauce through a fine-mesh sieve over the veal mixture. Heat the mixture over low heat, keeping the liquid just to a simmer.

- In another large skillet, melt the remaining 2 tablespoons of butter over moderate heat. Untie the pre-cooked vegetable bundles—leeks, celery, and asparagus—and add them to the skillet along with the carrots, turnips, fennel, and green beans. Cook just to warm them through, about 2 minutes. Season to taste with salt and pepper.

- To serve, place the veal mixture in a warmed deep serving platter. Arrange the garnish of vegetables on top and serve immediately.

YIELD: 6 TO 8 SERVINGS

Château de Bagnolet

Pot-au-Feu
(Boiled Beef Dinner)

This one-dish boiled beef dinner is popular in homes throughout the country. It is seldom on restaurant menus. I asked Château de Bagnolet, which is a region away from Paris, to serve up their pot-au-feu for *World Class Cuisine.* Pot-au-feu is popular all over France but especially in the Île de France region.

5	pounds lean short ribs, brisket, or chuck
1	knuckle of veal
	Salt and pepper
1	bay leaf
2	sprigs thyme
2	sprigs parsley
1	clove garlic
1	medium onion studded with 3 cloves
1	pound carrots, quartered
1	pound turnips, quartered

This Pot-au-Feu, made for World Class Cuisine *at the Hennessy family's Château de Bagnolet in Cognac, is a traditional French dish that is especially popular in the Île de France region.*

2	pounds leeks, white part only, tied into bunches
6	ribs celery, cut in half
1	pound white potatoes

2	pounds baking potatoes, such as russets, skins scrubbed
¾	to 1¼ cups whole milk
1	cup unsalted butter, chilled, cut into pieces
	Sea salt

🌿 🌿 🌿

- Place the beef in a large stockpot over high heat with enough water to cover by 3 inches. Bring the water to a boil. Skim off any foam that rises. Season with salt, about 1 teaspoon per quart. Sprinkle with a few grinds of black pepper. Skim again if necessary. Add all of the vegetables and herbs to the pot, except the potatoes. Bring to a gentle boil. Cover and cook over gentle heat for 3½ to 4 hours.
- Cook the potatoes separately in boiling salted water. Remove the beef and all of the vegetables from the stockpot and set them aside. Discard the herbs and veal knuckle. Let the stock rest for about 15 minutes. Then, reheat the stock and serve with the meat and vegetables.

YIELD: 6 SERVINGS

Le Parc Victor Hugo

Potato Purée

Although basic and homey, this simple mashed potato recipe is actually credited with helping to make Le Parc Hôtel's Joel Robuchon a famous chef. This version is actually a creamy, silky purée that is softened with a mountain of butter. The key here, says Chef Robuchon, is to buy uniformly sized potatoes and make sure the butter is well chilled.

🌿 🌿 🌿

- Place the unpeeled, whole potatoes in a large pot with 1 tablespoon of salt per quart of water. Simmer the potatoes, uncovered, over moderate heat until tender (when a knife inserted comes away easily, about 20 to 30 minutes). Drain the potatoes as soon as they are cooked.
- Meanwhile, in a large saucepan, bring the milk just to a boil over high heat. Set aside.
- As soon as the potatoes are cool enough to handle, peel them. Pass the potatoes through the finest grid of a food mill into a large, heavy-bottomed saucepan set over low heat. With a wooden spatula, stir the potatoes vigorously to dry them, 4 to 5 minutes. Now begin adding about 12 tablespoons of the butter, little by little, stirring vigorously until each batch of butter is thoroughly incorporated; the mixture should be fluffy and light. Then slowly add about three-fourths of the hot milk in a thin stream, stirring vigorously until the milk is incorporated.
- Pass the mixture through a flat fine-mesh sieve into another heavy-bottomed saucepan. Stir vigorously, and if the purée seems a bit heavy and stiff, add additional butter and milk, stirring all the while. Taste for seasoning.

YIELD: 6 TO 8 SERVINGS

Le Grand Vefour

Biscuit de Savoie with Lime and Ginger

A Savoy biscuit is actually a short sponge cake that has been made in France since 1348 when it was made for the court of Amadeus VI of Savoy, France. The cake is extremely light in texture, due to the large number of eggs. Le Grand Vefour has added a citrus flavoring to the traditional Savoy, one of many common variations to the basic recipe.

8	eggs, separated
1½	cups sugar, plus more for pan preparation
1	cup all-purpose flour
2	teaspoons cornmeal
¼	cup cornstarch
½	teaspoon grated fresh ginger
	Zest from 1 lime
¼	cup butter

❋ ❋ ❋

- Preheat the oven to 350°. In a large mixing bowl, whisk together the 8 egg yolks and 1 cup of the sugar until frothy and white. Add half of the flour, 1 teaspoon of the cornmeal, all but 1 teaspoon of the cornstarch, the lime zest, and the ginger. Set aside.
- In another bowl, beat the egg whites until stiff and add the remaining ½ cup of sugar. Beat half of the egg whites into the egg-yolk preparation. Then add the remaining flour and cornmeal, along with the rest of the cornstarch. Finish by adding the rest of the egg-white mixture.

- Butter and sugar a Savoy mold. Pour the mixture into the mold and bake for 45 minutes or until a tester inserted comes out clean. (Note: Turn the mold ⅛ turn every quarter hour.)

YIELD: 12 TO 14 SERVINGS

Le Marignan-Elysées

Gendarme de Saint-Tropez (Chocolate Policeman's Hat)

In honor of the French policeman's hat, this chocolate mousse cake stands sentinel at the table, ready for the eager palate.

FILLING:

2	cups heavy cream
1	vanilla bean, split lengthwise
¾	cup sugar
5	egg yolks

MOUSSE:

½	(scant) cup heavy cream
7	ounces good-quality chocolate
¼	cup butter, softened
1¼	cups heavy cream

BASE:

14	ounces good-quality chocolate, coarsely chopped

❋ ❋ ❋

The Chocolate Policeman's Hat

- Place the cream and vanilla bean in a small saucepan. Bring the mixture to a boil, then remove it from the heat.
- In a small bowl, whisk the sugar and egg yolks until the mixture thickens and turns pale yellow. Gradually whisk in half the cream and vanilla mixture, then the other half, and return it to the pan. Heat over a low flame until a custard forms and thickens. (Do not boil.)

- Remove the cream mixture from the heat and pass through a strainer into a medium bowl. Cover the custard with plastic wrap and let cool to room temperature; then transfer to the refrigerator to cool for 6 hours.
- To make the mousse, bring the cream to a boil in a saucepan, boiling for 1 minute. Remove the mixture from the heat and set it aside to cool from hot to warm.
- Melt the chocolate in the top of a double boiler. When the cream is warm, mix it into the chocolate. Leave to cool.
- In a large bowl, whisk the butter for 2 to 3 minutes until it turns pale. Still whisking, slowly add the chocolate cream and mix until smooth. Whip the cream, then fold it into the mousse.
- Melt the base chocolate in a double boiler. Spread it out onto an ungreased baking sheet to ¼-inch thickness. Once it has set, use a 3-inch biscuit cutter to cut 12 circles. Place 1 circle on each of 8 dessert plates. Spoon the mousse around the edge of the chocolate circles to make a ring with walls about 1½ inches thick. Spoon the chilled custard into the center of each ring and cover with a layer of the mousse. Using a knife, smooth down the top and sides.
- Cut the last 4 circles in half and arrange 1 in the center of each mousse to resemble the peak of the gendarme's cap. Chill before serving.

YIELD: 8 SERVINGS

BURGUNDY/RHÔNE VALLEY

Wine and Cheese Where a Famous Cuisinier Was Born

*A*lthough the name of an area of France, Burgundy is an evocative word that summons up images of rolling hills threaded with grapevines that have been growing for centuries. Burgundy is home of what is considered to be the world's most famous red wine. Its other claim to fame is that Dijon and Lyon rank as the unofficial gastronomic capitals of France. Parisian gourmets think nothing of getting in their cars and ambling down from Paris out into the country on a three-hour jaunt to eat lunch or dinner here.

Burgundy, located southeast of Paris, is mainly cattle country, with the traditional boeuf bourguignon heading the list of many beef dishes made with wine. The area is also well known for its escargot, considered in France as the symbol of eternal life. Freshwater trout is found in streams, and mushrooms and chèvre or goat cheese are produced here. Just as an aside, the country claims to produce some ninety different

Chef Michel Troisgros collects paintings from the Fauvist period for his museumlike restaurant and prepares masterpieces of his own, such as the Mussels and Radishes with Cucumbered Mustard. (See recipe on page 121.)

varieties of cheese made with goat's milk. Cow's milk cheeses are also made, the best known being *Epoisses*, which originated with Cistercian monks in the fifteenth century. The soft and creamy cheese has a golden/pinkish rind. *Fromage blanc* is a fine cream cheese used widely in desserts and also savories, and made in Bresse.

Dijon is the heart of Burgundy and is synonymous with the mustard by the same name but is also known for cassis, a liqueur made from the syrup of black currants and used in making sorbets and candies. In Lyon, farther south and slightly west of Dijon, quenelles or poached fish dumplings are the things people talk about. But they also converse about traditional and new dishes and all things food over small tabletop burners where cheese is melted and boiled potatoes are served for dipping.

Lyon is known for its charcuteries, which are a cross between a butcher shop and delicatessen. Wonderful sausages are made and sold at charcuteries.

But Burgundy produced another gastronomic notable of a different kind. Jean-Anthelme Brillat-Savarin was born here in 1755. Today he is quoted throughout the world for his writings on food. He was insightful and passionate and perhaps best summed up what is really in the hearts of men when he wrote, "The discovery of a new dish means more for the happiness of mankind than the discovery of a star."

Troisgros

Baked Tomatoes Stuffed with Almonds, Anchovies, and Roasted Peppers

Pleasant as an appetizer, this is also a sumptuous garnish that may be added to most any French main course. Serve with a glass of Burgundy wine from this famous region and a salad, and you have a luncheon special.

TOMATOES:

8	ripe medium tomatoes, peeled and cored
8	fresh thyme stalks
	Salt and pepper
	Extra virgin olive oil

STUFFING:

2	red bell peppers, roasted and finely diced
12	whole almonds, coarsely chopped
2	anchovies (not those preserved in oil, but anchovies preserved in salt)
40	capers
1	small garlic clove, minced
	Red wine vinegar
	Hot pepper sauce

GARNISH:

8	sprigs each: basil, chervil, chives, thyme
6	pitted black olives

- Preheat the oven to 250°. Create a cavity in each tomato by expanding the hole made to core the tomato. Remove some of the tomato pulp and the seeds but be sure there is enough body and weight to the tomatoes that they can stand on their own. Sprinkle the leaves of each stalk of thyme into each tomato. Season each with salt and pepper. Place the tomatoes in a baking dish and add enough olive oil to cover the tomatoes almost ¾ of the way up the sides. Bake the tomatoes for 3 hours in the slow oven.
- In a medium-sized mixing bowl, mix the roasted red peppers, almonds, anchovies, capers, garlic, 1 generous tablespoon of olive oil, 1 generous tablespoon of vinegar, and 4 drops of hot pepper sauce. Toss and mix well.

Wine Suggestion

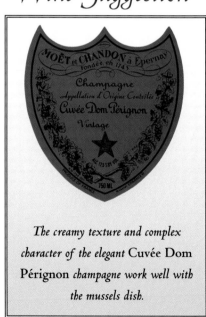

The creamy texture and complex character of the elegant Cuvée Dom Pérignon *champagne work well with the mussels dish.*

- Remove the tomatoes from the oven and stuff them with the spicy stuffing mixture.
- To serve, place 2 tomatoes onto each plate upside down. Decorate each plate with the sprigs of basil, chervil, chives, and thyme. Drizzle with olive oil. Cut the olives into petal shapes and add to the plate as a garnish.

YIELD: 4 SERVINGS

Troisgros

Mussels and Radishes with Cucumbered Mustard and Curried Cream Sauce

If you are lucky enough to get your hands on real Dijon mustard, what a treat. Otherwise, most Dijon mustards sold in the United States are marked Dijon-style, as they are not made in Dijon. Nonetheless, Dijon-style mustard contains most of the same ingredients—brown mustard seeds, white wine, unfermented grape juice, and a blend of seasonings.

MUSSELS AND CURRY SAUCE:

1	cup white wine
1	onion, finely chopped
1	sprig of thyme
1	bay leaf
2	pounds mussels
1	teaspoon curry powder
½	cup plus 2 tablespoons heavy cream
	Sea salt and ground pepper
	Juice of 1 lime

CUCUMBER:

1	medium cucumber
1	teaspoon Dijon-style mustard
1	tablespoon olive oil
1	tablespoon chopped dill

GARNISH:

| 24 | red radishes, cut julienne |

- Combine the white wine, onion, thyme, and bay leaf in a Dutch oven. Over high heat, bring the wine and spices to a boil. Add the mussels. Reduce the heat and stir frequently until the mussels have opened. Remove from the heat, and, using a slotted spoon, remove the mussels from their shells.
- Strain the cooking liquid through a sieve and into a small saucepan. Over high heat, cook the liquid, slowly adding the curry and the heavy cream. Bring to a boil and season with the salt and pepper to taste. Remove the curried cream from the heat and stir in the lime juice. Refrigerate until thoroughly chilled.
- Meanwhile, cut the cucumber into 2-inch rounds. Sprinkle the cucumber with salt and let stand for 15 minutes. Rinse the slices with water and drain well. Combine the cucumber with the mustard, olive oil, dill, and black pepper.
- To serve, arrange the mussels decoratively around the rim of a serving plate. Place a sliver of radish on each mussel. Make a nest of the cucumbers in the center of the plate. Remove the bay leaf from the curry sauce and drape the sauce over each plate.

YIELD: 6 SERVINGS

Troisgros

Sunflower Meringues with Passion-Fruit Sauce

What can be more delightful, set out onto a plate, than an edible bunch of sunflowers? Well, you cannot eat sunflowers, but dreams can come true with the chef's decorative dessert. You will no doubt enjoy making this dish that looks too good to eat.

Passion fruit was not just named for its romantic implications—considered to be seductively sweet—but also for how parts of the fruit's flowers resemble different symbols of Christ's crucifixion, such as the crown of thorns. Though native to Brazil, passion fruit is also grown in California and Florida.

MERINGUE:

4	egg whites
½	cup plus 2 tablespoons sugar
1	cup confectioners' sugar

CREAM:

1	cup milk
1	vanilla bean
2	egg yolks
½	cup sugar
3	tablespoons cornstarch

SAUCE:

16	whole passion fruits (about 4½ pounds)
1-2	tablespoons sugar

ASSEMBLY:

1	cup heavy cream, whipped

- Begin by preparing the meringue. Place the egg whites and the sugars over a double boiler. Whip until the mixture reaches 140° or until it is hot to the touch. Remove the mixture from the heat and beat until the mixture becomes cold and thick.

- Preheat the oven to 200°. Line a baking sheet with waxed paper. Grease the paper. Using a pastry bag, make 8 round circles, 6 inches in diameter, onto the baking sheet, about ½-inch apart. Use the pastry bag to create petals and the stem of a flower for each one. Bake the meringues in the oven for 1 hour. Remove the meringues from the oven when just a hint of golden color appears. Another indication of doneness is that they will release easily from the paper. Allow to cool slightly and then remove from the baking sheet. Set aside.

- In a medium saucepan over medium-high heat, bring the milk and the vanilla bean to a boil. Meanwhile, combine the egg yolks and sugar in a large mixing bowl. Add the cornstarch and beat until light and fluffy. Remove the vanilla bean from the milk and pour 2 tablespoons or so of the hot milk into the egg mixture. This helps the mixture adjust to the hot milk and prevents the eggs from scrambling. Then, add the rest of the hot milk. Cook until the cream is thick, stirring constantly. Set aside.

- Prepare the sauce. Slice the fruit and remove the pulp. Strain the pulp to remove the seeds. Place the pulp in a medium saucepan with the sugar. Cook the mixture over medium heat until it is reduced by half. It should be syrupy.

- To assemble, place a meringue flower onto an individual serving plate. Garnish the flower with the whipped cream and top with the cooked fruit mixture. Spoon some additional fruit mixture around the flowers.

YIELD: 8 SERVINGS

FLANDERS

ARTOIS

PICARDY

NORMANDY

ILE DE FRANCE

CHAMPAGNE

LORRAINE

ALSACE

BRITTANY

MAINE

ORLÉANAIS

FRANCHE COMTÉ

ANJOU

TOUR-AINE

BERRY

NIVER-NAIS

BURGUNDY

POITOU

BOUR-BONNAIS

AUNIS

ANGOU-MOIS

MARCHE

AUVERGNE

LYON-NAIS

SAINTONGE

● BORDEAUX
AND
THE
ATLANTIC
COAST

DAUPHINÉ

GUYENNE

COMTAT

PROVENCE

GASCONY

LANGUEDOC

BEARN

FOIX

ROUSSILON

PROVENCE

❦ ❦ ❦

Boules, Boulangeries, Love Apples, and a Place Where the Bread Man Still Delivers

Maybe all the rush of excitement and commotion over this rural area of France known as Provence in recent years has set us all to daydreaming and fantasizing. But once you set foot on Provençal soil you can indeed feel the earth energize and the soul and spirit lift. Provence is everything you may have heard about it. And discovering this gentle, peaceful, thrilling land through its cuisine is even more sensual than just poking about its red-tiled roofs and the cypress trees that help block the famous mistral winds.

A meal in Provence often begins with a tasty tapenade, a pastelike spread usually made with capers, olives, anchovies, olive oil, lemon juice, and a variety of other condiments, and eaten on crusty bread, often rubbed with garlic. Sometimes the tapenade is eaten as a snack accompanied by the region's well-known apéritif called pastis. The pale green, anise-based drink seems nearly as common as drinking water.

Vegetables and herbs constitute the main diet of the Provençal people. Theirs

Artist Georges Flanet captures the colors of Provence on canvas in St. Tropez.

is a colorful menu with a palette of vegetables as broad as those of the region's myriad painters. Especially popular are the zucchini, saffron, bell peppers, and tomatoes (widely known as love apples here) that crop up in minigardens. Everyone in Provence seems to have a green thumb. Meals are usually concluded with fruit and lots of fresh goat cheese. Also made here, in an area called Montélimar, is a candy or nougat made of honey, sugar, eggs, almonds, pistachios, and vanilla.

Overall, the cuisine is based on lots of garlic, tomatoes, and olive oil. Dishes à la Provençal are often made with this combination as well as with onions, olives, mushrooms, and anchovies. Provençal cooking is pungently spiced with herbs and it is from here we get herbes de Provence, a blend of basil, fennel seed, lavender, marjoram, rosemary, sage, summer savory, and thyme. (Use this blend to season any of your meat, poultry, or vegetable dishes.)

It is no surprise, either, that Provence would host a multitude of open-air markets. Provence is a bustle of activity during market hours. While shoppers pick the day's freshest, a bread man is making his

Cheese vendor Gille Pellegrino shows off his products at the lively market that takes place weekly in St. Remy.

rounds somewhere in his telltale van, carting crusty rounds and baguettes made at the area's many boulangeries or bakeries. Meanwhile, men with an eye for sport are pitting wits at boules, where you will hear the thud and click of steel balls on soft dirt.

Lavender is a big industry in Provence, so fields of purple often dance in the countryside winds. The crop is harvested for soap, for decorating dining tables, for stuffing into cushions, and for seasoning food.

The people of this delightful area are as jovial and fiery as the bountiful land that produces such great variety in fervent abundance. They revel in discussions about everything from the best way to travel to the market to how to make bouillabaisse, salade niçoise, or brandade. The Provençal people love to talk about everyday life and especially their food. So here are a few recipes to help you see why, and to help you re-create their lifestyle at home.

Château de la Messardière

Chilled Melon and Grapefruit in a Mint-and-Ginger Sauce

I love Chef Jean-Louis Vosgien's poetic description of this dish, "You will enjoy this as a light appetizer . . . on a terrace, in the shade of a tree. . . ." It seems to transport you right to the sultry countryside of Provence in summertime. The chef calls for using palm sugar in the syrup for this dish. Also known as jaggery, the sugar is unrefined, dark, and coarse. It is made from palm trees and offers a sweet, winelike flavor to any dish. You can purchase palm sugar in East Indian markets, or substitute with raw, unrefined sugar pieces. Even white granulated sugar will do, if necessary.

SAUCE:

1	cup grapefruit juice
1	cup palm sugar or dark, unrefined sugar pieces
¾	cup fresh lemon juice
2	tablespoons diced crystallized ginger

FRUIT:

2	pounds any combination or single variety of a muskmelon such as cantaloupe
4	medium grapefruits
10	leaves mint, cut into thin slices, plus 4 small mint bouquets for garnish

The avid boules players of St. Tropez gather daily for sport in Place Carnot.

Château de la Messardière

Orange Soup with Spices

Easy to prepare, this wonderful appetizer or dessert soup can be customized to your individual tastes. Chef Jean-Louis Vosgien says "be adventurous." Keep the soup basic but add your own spice mixture, including such treats as cardamon or saffron.

2	pints orange juice
6	whole cloves
½	vanilla bean
1	teaspoon coarsely ground white pepper
1	cinnamon stick
3	peeled orange segments
2	slices kiwi fruit
½	pint strawberries, cut into quarters

- In a medium saucepan, warm the grapefruit, sugar, and the lemon juice until the sugar is dissolved. Do not boil. Add the ginger and refrigerate until chilled.
- To serve this dish, scoop out the melons using a melon baller or cut the melon into a ½-inch dice. Peel and cut the grapefruits into segments, removing them from the skin and stirring the juice into the sauce. Evenly divide the melon and grapefruit sections onto 4 individual serving plates.
- Cover the fruits with the sauce and sprinkle with the chiffonade of mint. Garnish with a sprig of mint.

YIELD: 4 SERVINGS

- In a medium saucepan, bring the orange juice to a boil. Remove the juice from the heat. Stir in the cloves, the vanilla bean, pepper, and the cinnamon stick. Allow the spices to marinate in the juice in the refrigerator until the mixture cools, about 45 minutes to 1 hour.
- Strain the soup and spoon into individual soup bowls. Add the orange, kiwi, and strawberries.

YIELD: 4 SERVINGS

Gazpacho with Lobster-and-Bell-Pepper Timbales

Gazpacho simply means a purée of vegetables that becomes a soup. This recipe incorporates that basic gazpacho premise along with a mixture of bell peppers and lobster meat that is molded and placed in the center of the soup. No question that this can be a meal in itself. It is picture-perfect and no so difficult to do. If necessary, substitute the fish stock of your choice for lobster broth.

LOBSTER STOCK:

2	tablespoons butter
2	carrots, cut into ½-inch pieces
4	pearl onions, cut into ½-inch pieces
2	leeks, white part only, cut into ½-inch pieces
1	sprig fresh thyme
1	bay leaf
1¼	pound lobster

VEGETABLE PURÉE:

1	large English cucumber, peeled, cut in half, and seeded
1	rib celery, cut into a medium dice
1	red bell pepper, seeded and diced
1	yellow bell pepper, seeded and diced
1	green bell pepper, seeded and diced
2	ripe tomatoes, cut into quarters and then into eighths
1	small yellow onion, diced
¼	cup heavy cream, plus 2 tablespoons

	Salt and pepper
1	slice white bread
2	tablespoons mayonnaise
2	tablespoons vegetable oil

TIMBALES:

½	green bell pepper
½	red bell pepper
½	yellow bell pepper
1	tablespoon fresh lemon juice
1	tablespoon olive oil, plus more for drizzling

- Prepare the lobster broth. Bring 1 quart of water to a boil. Meanwhile, in a small skillet, heat the butter and sauté the vegetables until they sweat. Add the vegetables to the boiling water and drop in the lobster. Cook the lobster about 5 minutes. Remove the lobster from the water and set aside to cool, leaving the vegetables to simmer with the heat off.
- Make the vegetable purée. In a food processor, toss together half of the cucumber (reserving the other half for later), the celery, half of the diced peppers (reserving the other half for later), the tomatoes, onion, and ¼ cup of the heavy cream. Add the bread slice and season with salt and pepper. Whirl together. Then add the mayonnaise and blend again. Add the vegetable oil, just to incorporate, and the lobster stock. Strain the mixture. Place it in the refrigerator.
- Return to the cooled lobster and break up the shell. Remove the meat, setting aside the meat of the large claw and the tail for the timbales. Cut the remaining meat into a fine dice. Add the reserved diced bell peppers to the lobster meat. Toss together with the lemon juice and olive oil. Season with salt and pepper. Set aside and prepare the timbales.
- Slice the reserved half of the English cucumber into paper-thin slices to be used for lining a 3-

inch ring mold. Carefully line the mold with plastic wrap. Coat the inside of the mold lightly with olive oil. Carefully line the mold with cucumber slices, overlapping the slices as you go. Place the bell pepper and lobster mixture in the center of the mold, pressing gently with the back of a spoon so that the lobster mixture holds its shape. Invert the timbale into a rim-soup bowl, removing the ring.

- Cut the reserved lobster tail meat into round disks and place them on top of the timbale. Slice the meat of the large claw in half horizontally and then place it on top of the timbale. Remove the gazpacho from the refrigerator and strain it into the bowl around the timbale, using a fine-mesh strainer.

YIELD: 2 SERVINGS

The Gazpacho with Lobster-and-Bell-Pepper Timbales rests on a ledge overlooking the gardens at the Royal Riviera in St. Jean du Cap Ferrat.

Warm Vegetable Salad on Olive Oil Tarts with Fennel and White Wine Sauce

A moist dough made with olive oil creates an edible platter for this salad of soft lettuces warmed and dressed with a tasty blend of Provençal ingredients. In my family (as I mentioned in the introduction to the Provence region) we also talked at length about food. This would have been one of those dishes to spark a lively conversation.

TART:

1¼	cups all-purpose flour
2	tablespoons extra virgin olive oil
¼	cup plus 1 tablespoon water
	Salt

VEGETABLES:

2	tablespoons extra virgin olive oil
12	red baby radishes
8	baby carrots with leaves
8	young fennel bulbs (should be very small)
2	small zucchini, cut into ½-inch pieces
8	spring onions (white and green parts), chopped

SAUCE:

½	scant cup white wine vinegar
1	cup quality white wine
4	cups chicken stock or broth
	Freshly ground black pepper

	Sprinkle each of: fresh or dried cilantro and thyme
	Sprinkle of dried fennel
	Zest of 1 small lemon

ASSEMBLY:

½	cup arugula
½	cup mesclun
1	cup cured ewe's cheese or Mozzarella
1	Comice pear, cut in thin slices
	Olive oil for drizzling

- In a large bowl, mix together the flour, olive oil, water, and salt and form into a soft paste. Let it rest at room temperature for 30 minutes. Preheat the oven to 400°. When the dough has rested, roll it out to about an 18-inch rectangle. Cut 4 6-inch rounds and place on a greased baking sheet. Bake for 10 minutes or until golden brown.

- Heat the olive oil in a large skillet and while the tarts bake, cook the carrots, radishes, fennel, zucchini, and onions over medium-high heat until browned. Deglaze the pan with the white wine vinegar and the white wine. Allow the mixture to reduce by half and then add the chicken stock. Cook the mixture until it reduces by half again. Add the black pepper, cilantro, thyme, dried fennel, and the lemon juice. Continue cooking over medium-high heat until the sauce reaches a thick consistency.

- Add 1 teaspoon of olive oil to a sauté pan and heat over a medium flame. Sauté the arugula and mesclun just long enough to wilt.

- To assemble the dish, arrange the arugula and mesclun evenly among the 4 tarts. Evenly divide the pear slices over the lettuces. Follow with the warm vegetables and the ewe's cheese. Sprinkle with the olive oil and salt and pepper. Serve immediately.

YIELD: 4 SERVINGS

Château de la Messardière

Mussel and Salmon Soup with Saffron

3	pounds mussels
1	pint water
2	cloves garlic
1	medium onion
2	shallots
¼	cup butter
1	cup white wine
2	cups heavy cream
⅛	teaspoon saffron, or just a few threads
	Salt and pepper
2	ounces broccoli (tops only), blanched
2	ounces smoked salmon, diced

- Clean and wash the mussels in fresh water. Cook them over high heat, covered in the water. Remove them from their shells. Set aside, including the shells.
- Slice the garlic, onion, and shallots. In a medium skillet, melt the butter and sweat the vegetables for about 2 minutes. Add the wine; bring to a boil. Add the reserved stock from the mussels, the cream, and the mussel shells. Cook for 25 minutes over low heat. Strain the soup and transfer to another pot. Bring the soup to the boil; add the saffron; boil 5 minutes more and season with salt and pepper to taste. Purée the soup, if necessary, just until smooth. Evenly divide the mussels and broccoli into 4 soup bowls. Pour in the soup and top with the diced salmon.

YIELD: 4 SERVINGS

Each spring . . . the landscape can be seen to sprout with an altogether different crop—still quiet figures. . . . They have easels and quivers filled with brushes and crayons. They wear hats and frowns of concentration. They seem to be hypnotized by distance until, with sudden pecks of the brush, they set to work committing Provence to canvas.

—Peter Mayle, *Provence*

The vegetable gazpacho is the main ingredient for a picnic on the grounds of Domaine de Valmouriane in St. Remy. (See recipe on next page.)

Domaine de Valmouriane

Provençal Vegetable Gazpacho with Basil and Langoustines

If you want a refreshing, tasty soup for lunch or as an appetizer, this unusual, very thick soup will fit the bill. It is almost like whisking the garden to your table in a bowl.

1	pound ripe tomatoes, seeded
2	red bell peppers, seeds and membrane removed and peppers coarsely chopped
2	green bell peppers, seeds and membrane removed and peppers coarsely chopped
3	cucumbers, peeled, seeded, and coarsely chopped
2	shallots or scallions (white part only), chopped
1	small onion, coarsely chopped
1	bulb fennel, bottom only, coarsely chopped
	Salt and pepper
½	cup balsamic vinegar
½	cup plus 2 tablespoons olive oil
12	cooked langoustines
1	small bouquet red and green basil

- In a blender or food processor, purée the tomatoes, peppers, cucumbers, shallots, onion, fennel, and salt and pepper until a paste forms. Mix in the vinegar and olive oil. Place the paste in the refrigerator until ready to serve.
- Meanwhile, heat the 2 tablespoons of olive oil in a sauté pan and cook the langoustines until heated through, about 5 minutes.
- Place the chilled soup in individual serving bowls and evenly divide the langoustines among the dishes. Garnish with the basil.

YIELD: 4 SERVINGS

Wine Suggestion

Strawberry-like fruit and creamy texture make this perfectly dry rosé— from the Tuscan Estates of Ruffino—a lively and flavorful accompaniment to the Provençal vegetable gazpacho.

La Bastide de Moustiers

Braised Beet and Cabbage Casserole with Country Bacon

I love this dish because it includes beets and cabbage. Here, these vegetables are accompanied by carrots, potatoes, and a generous amount of onions. Look for an Irish-style (more like a ham) or Canadian bacon. Ceps (known in Italy as porcini) are wild mushrooms that have a smooth, meaty texture and woody flavor. Use dried ceps (reconstituted) if fresh are unavailable.

8-	ounce slab country-style or Canadian bacon, cut into large dice
2	whole cloves garlic
3	large carrots, cut into large pieces
12	small new potatoes, skins cleaned
15	baby onions
8	ounces ceps, cut in half
8	ounces fresh beets, peeled and cut in large pieces
1	cup chicken stock
1½	cups (12 ounces) green cabbage leaves, cut in half
	Salt and freshly ground pepper
2	teaspoons olive oil

- In a medium skillet, brown the bacon and garlic over medium-high heat. When the bacon has browned, add the carrots, potatoes, onions, ceps, and beets. Lightly braise the vegetables. When browned, add the chicken stock and turn the heat down to low. Simmer the vegetables until fork tender, about 10 minutes to 15 minutes. Add the cabbage and season the vegetables with salt and pepper. Add the olive oil. Serve immediately.

YIELD: 4 SERVINGS

St. Tropez and the French Riviera beyond

Royal Riviera

Filet of Fish with Spring-Vegetable Cream Sauce and Dried Tomatoes

The Royal Riviera prepares this simple dish in its kitchen on the Riviera, with a fish called John Dory (Jean-doré). John Dory, a very popular fish in Europe, is identified by black spots on its skin, said to be the thumbprints of Saint Peter. Saint Peter, or Saint Pierre (as the fish is also called), was said to have thrown the fish back in the water after it was caught because the fish was moaning (something the fish does whenever it is out of water.)

*W*ine *Suggestion*

SIMI

Chardonnay

MENDOCINO COUNTY 29%
SONOMA COUNTY 58%
NAPA COUNTY 13%

750 ml.   ALC. 13.4% BY VOL.

The full-bodied Simi Chardonnay *provides the rich fruit complexity and balance needed to marry well with the filet of fish and its cream sauce.*

You may substitute flounder or filet of sole if John Dory is not available. But be sure to use young spring vegetables for this recipe.

2½	pounds John Dory filets, or substitute with flounder or sole
1	tablespoon plus ¼ cup olive oil
1	quart fish stock
2	shallots, finely chopped
1	rib celery, diced
1	sprig thyme
1	bay leaf
1½	cups white wine
	Sea salt
1	baby fennel bulb and stalks, sliced
1	cup pearl onions
2	baby artichoke hearts, freshened with a squeeze of lemon juice
2	carrots, cut into disks
1	baby zucchini, sliced into disks
2	stalks white asparagus, woody ends snapped off
1	cup small broccoli florets
1	cup chanterelle mushrooms, rinsed and dried
¼	cup heavy cream
¼	cup butter, softened
	Dried tomatoes for garnish
	Sprigs of fresh chives

- Place the John Dory into a medium nonstick saucepan. Sauté the fish in the 1 tablespoon olive oil, fleshside down, to avoid curling up when cooked. (Do not cook on the reverse side unless substituting with flounder or sole.) Set aside.
- In a medium skillet, add the fish stock, the shallots, celery, thyme, the bay leaf, and 1 cup of the white wine. Season to taste with sea salt. Place the saucepan over medium heat and cook until reduced by half.

- Meanwhile, in a medium saucepan, heat the ¼ cup olive oil over medium-high heat. When the oil is hot, add the fennel stalks, onions, artichoke hearts, carrots, and zucchini. Sauté the vegetables until tender and slightly crisp. Set aside, keeping them warm.
- Strain the fish broth and place it in a small pan to reduce a little more over medium-high heat. Add the asparagus, broccoli, and chanterelles. Add the ½ cup white wine and cook until the liquid is reduced by ½ (about ¾ cup). When the liquid has reduced, pour in the white wine and the butter.
- Once the butter has melted and is well incorporated, place the asparagus, broccoli, carrots, and fennel around the dish. Place the filet in the center and drizzle the sauce all around. Garnish with several dried tomatoes and sprigs of fresh chives.

YIELD: 4 SERVINGS

Domaine de Valmouriane

Red Mullet with Zucchini Blossoms and Mint Sauce

4	filets of red mullet, boned (about 2 pounds) (bones reserved)
2	tablespoons vegetable oil

SAUCE:

3½	ounces (7 tablespoons) butter
2	shallots, finely chopped
1	small bunch mint, all chopped, except for a few leaves for garnish
2½	cups white wine

ZUCCHINI:

4	zucchini blossoms, pistils removed

- Prepare the basis for the sauce by making a fish stock. In a large skillet, heat 4 tablespoons of the butter over medium-high heat. Add the bones and the shallots and the chopped mint. Stir and add the white wine. Allow the stock to cook for about 20 minutes over medium heat.
- While the stock is cooking, steam the zucchini blossoms for a few minutes, cooking until tender but still crisp. Drain on a tea towel and carefully fan out the blossoms. Keep the flowers warm.
- Meanwhile, add the cream to the fish stock and boil over medium-high heat for about 5 minutes. Add the remaining butter, a few pieces at a time, stirring well to incorporate.
- In a large skillet, heat about 2 tablespoons of vegetable oil and quickly cook the fish over medium-high heat, 2 minutes on each side.
- To serve, strain the sauce and pool some of it onto the bottom of each individual serving plate. Divide the fish evenly among the plates, placing the mullet on top of the sauce. Garnish with the zucchini blossom fans and mint.

YIELD: 4 SERVINGS

Château de la Messardière

Cod and Oysters with Artichokes and Tandoori Sauce

Chef Jean-Louis Vosgien considers this dish "an amusing marriage" of ingredients. True, it is entertaining, and delicious, too. If you feel that the tandoori spices may be a little too hot, substitute with milder spices of your choice and season a bit heavier with salt and pepper. Create your own culinary nuptials with this dish.

2	tablespoons clarified butter
	Salt and pepper
4	cod filets (skin on), about 4 ounces each
4	artichoke hearts (if using fresh, boil them; if from a can, use the unmarinated ones)
4	dried tomatoes, cut julienne
12	large oysters
2	tablespoons butter
1	tablespoon tandoori spices
¼	cup chicken stock or broth
½	cup oyster juice
1	small bunch fresh coriander, chopped, for garnish

* Heat the clarified butter in a skillet. Season the cod to taste with salt and pepper. Pan-fry the fish in the skillet about 5 minutes on each side or until lightly browned and cooked through. Remove the fish from the skillet but keep warm. Add the artichoke hearts and the dried tomatoes to the skillet and a little more clarified butter if

Wine Suggestion

CASA LAPOSTOLLE
SAUVIGNON BLANC
COLCHAGUA

750 ML.   PRODUCED AND BOTTLED IN CHILE BY CASA LAPOSTOLLE S.A.   ALC. 12% BY VOL

This wine—from **Casa Lapostolle** *in Chile—has a rich texture; fresh, ripe fruit flavor; and the characteristic smoky, flinty taste of the Sauvignon Blanc grape. This makes it a perfect match for the cod and oysters recipe.*

necessary. Sauté the artichokes and tomatoes over medium heat, cooking until the artichokes are lightly browned.
* Meanwhile, remove the oysters from their shells and set aside.
* In another smaller skillet, heat the 2 tablespoons of butter and sweat the tandoori spices. Add the chicken broth and the oyster juice and boil the liquids in the pan for about 2 minutes. Add the remaining butter and continue boiling the liquid and spices gently. Season with salt and a little pepper. Add the oysters to the liquid and poach for 5 minutes.
* To serve, place each of the cod filets on individual serving plates. Place the oysters on top, followed by the artichokes and tomatoes. Drizzle with pan juices and the tandoori sauce. Garnish with the coriander.

YIELD: 4 SERVINGS

Roast Leg of Suckling Pig with Caramelized Pears, Potatoes, and Turnips

GRAVY:

	Pork trimmings from 1 leg of suckling pig (see pig ingredients)
3	cloves garlic, finely chopped
1	medium onion, thinly sliced

PIG:

1	leg suckling pig (3½ to 4 pounds)
	Salt and pepper

VEGETABLES:

2	firm pears
2	large white potatoes
8	medium round turnips
2	tablespoons olive oil

Wine Suggestion

RUFFINO

RISERVA DUCALE

Chianti Classico
DENOMINAZIONE DI ORIGINE CONTROLLATA
E GARANTITA
Riserva

BOTTLED BY
I. L. RUFFINO
PONTASSIEVE · ITALIA · 126/FI

750 ml ℮   ALCOHOL
                  13% BY VOL

The rich concentration of fruit and excellent structure in this Chianti Classico Riserva Gold Label, from the Tuscan firm of Ruffino, have made this wine a classic match to all meats, especially game and pork.

- Begin the recipe by making the gravy. Trim the leg of pork, reserving the trimmings to make a gravy. Make the gravy by placing the pork trimmings in a medium sauté pan over medium-high heat. Add the garlic and the onion. Season with salt and pepper and cook until the onions are browned. When browned, reduce the heat to a low simmer; add enough water to cover the onions and ½ inch above. Allow the mixture to reduce for about 2 hours.

- Meanwhile, prepare the roast leg of pig. Season the leg with salt and pepper and place it on a spit over an open fire for 45 minutes, or, cook en cocotte in the oven (in a casserole with a lid) at 350° for 1 hour or until crispy on the outside and browned well.

- Preheat the oven to 350° (or use the same oven the pig is roasting in). Cut the pears and pota- toes into ½-inch slices. Cut the turnips in half. In a large sauté pan, heat the olive oil and add the pears, potatoes, and turnips. Sauté until browned. Transfer the vegetables to a baking dish. Baste with the pork gravy. Bake in the oven for 15 to 20 minutes to tenderize and caramelize. Continue to baste the vegetables a few more times with the pork gravy.

- To serve, cut the leg into thick slices and serve with the caramelized vegetables and any leftover pork gravy.

YIELD: 4 SERVINGS

Stuffed Chicken en Croûte with Asparagus and Port Wine Sauce

Asparagus grows everywhere in Provence. This dish has the chef's oriental influence with a delicate taste and texture.

STUFFING:

4	chicken wings, skinned and boned
2	chicken legs, skinned and boned
1	teaspoon tandoori spices
1	tablespoon all-purpose flour
2	tablespoons Chinese oyster sauce
	Salt and pepper
¼	head Chinese cabbage, finely diced
	Butter for sautéing

CHICKEN BREASTS:

4	chicken breasts, skinned and boned
8	leaves phyllo dough, cut 2½ x 8 inches
2	tablespoons butter, melted

SAUCE:

2	tablespoons red port wine
¼	cup chicken stock
2	tablespoons butter

ASSEMBLY:

1	pound green asparagus, boiled

- Make the stuffing. Cut the chicken into small, bite-size pieces. Mix the chicken wings and legs with the tandoori spices, flour, and oyster sauce. Add salt and pepper to taste (be careful as the oyster sauce is salty). In a large skillet, sauté the chicken over a high flame until slightly crispy. Remove the chicken from the heat.

- In another pan, quickly sauté the cabbage in a little butter just until firm. Mix it in with the chicken. Set aside and prepare the chicken breasts.

- Make a large slit (pocket) in the chicken breasts and evenly distribute the filling into each breast. Cover the meat with the phyllo dough. (You will cover each piece of chicken with 2 leaves of phyllo dough.) Brush the first layer of the dough with butter and layer on a second piece. Brush again and wrap the phyllo around the stuffed chicken, brushing with more butter to seal and

Wine Suggestion

This is a rich, full-bodied wine that combines the bright fruit of the classic Tuscan Sangiovese grape with the complex flavors and lush texture of the Cabernet Sauvignon. Cabreo Il Borgo, from the Tuscan Estates of Ruffino, perfectly complements the Stuffed Chicken en Croûte.

also to help brown. Repeat with all pieces of chicken. Brown the chicken in a pan over medium-high heat for about 10 to 12 minutes.

- Meanwhile, prepare the port wine sauce. Bring the wine to a boil in a small saucepan. Add the chicken stock and let the sauce cook moderately for about 2 minutes. Add the 2 tablespoons of butter and allow the sauce to boil until the butter is melted. Season with salt and pepper to taste.

- To assemble the dish, place a chicken breast in the center of an individual serving plate. Add a few asparagus spears, with the woody ends tucked under the chicken, so that they fan out from the chicken. Drape some sauce over all and serve.

YIELD: 4 SERVINGS

La Bastide de Moustiers

Roast Herb-Scented Hen in a Spinach Gravy

A delicious paste of herbs, blended with butter and spread under the folds of the bird's skin, makes this an aromatic entrée.

¾	cup fresh herbs: rosemary, thyme, basil, chives, parsley
1	cup (2 sticks) butter
	Salt and pepper
1	free range hen (about 4½ pounds), ready for roasting
2	tablespoons butter
2	tablespoons all-purpose flour
1	cup milk
	Olive oil
1	clove garlic
2	pounds fresh spinach

- Preheat the oven to 350°. Chiffonade the herbs and mix them with the 1 cup of butter to form a paste. Season with salt and pepper. Lift the skin of the hen and spread the herb paste underneath. Place the hen in a roasting pan and bake for 40 minutes or until golden brown.

- Meanwhile, make a white sauce as a basis for the spinach gravy. Melt the 2 tablespoons of butter in a medium saucepan. Add the flour and stir well. Season with salt and pepper. Add the milk all at once to avoid any lumps. Stir well until the mixture is smooth and incorporated.

- Heat the olive oil in a sauté pan. Add the garlic and the spinach. Season with salt and pepper and cook for about 2 or 3 minutes, just until the garlic sweats and the spinach wilts. Pour the white sauce into the spinach and heat through. Mix with a few tablespoons of pan-gravy drippings from the hen dish. Place the hen in the center of a serving platter, surrounded with the gravy, and serve.

YIELD: 4 SERVINGS

Wine Suggestion

This full-bodied **Chianti Classico** *harmonizes with the rich flavors of the roast hen.*

1	tablespoon grated fresh ginger
	Juice of ½ lemon
3	tablespoons soy sauce
¼	cup sesame oil
	Salt and pepper

- Grill the bass under a broiler for 6 to 7 minutes, or until cooked tender. Keep warm and make the sauce.
- In a medium skillet, sweat the onions in the vegetable oil until just translucent, being careful to keep them firm, almost raw. Remove the pan from the heat. Add the tomatoes, ginger, lemon juice, soy sauce, sesame oil, and a little salt and freshly ground pepper. Season the fish with salt and pepper and serve with sauce.

YIELD: 4 SERVINGS

The Filet of Sea Bass in Sesame Sauce at Château de la Messardière in St. Tropez

Château de la Messardière

Filet of Sea Bass in Sesame Sauce

Light and fragrant, this dish is so simple to prepare and the results are astonishing.

BASS:

| 4 | 5-ounce sea bass filets |

SAUCE:

4	green onions, tops removed and discarded
2	tablespoons vegetable oil
1	diced tomato, skin removed

Château de la Messardière

Lamb Chops with Olive Paste, Capers, and Lime Syrup

Chef Jean-Louis Vosgien suggests serving this dish with spring vegetables such as artichokes, garden peas, baby carrots, and young turnips. The olive paste offers a decidely Provençal flair.

SYRUP:

	Skin of 1 lime
½	pint water
¾	cup sugar

LAMB:

12	lamb chops
	Salt and pepper
2	tablespoons vegetable oil

SAUCE:

2	ounces lamb stock (see page 184)
1	tablespoon capers
1	teaspoon black olive paste
2	teaspoons lime juice

ASSEMBLY:

| 1 | teaspoon chopped fresh chives |
| 2 | small bunches chervil |

- Peel the skin from the lime and julienne the skin. Reserve the lime for later use. Bring the

The Stuffed Chicken en Croûte poolside in St. Tropez at Château de la Messardière (See recipe on page 138.)

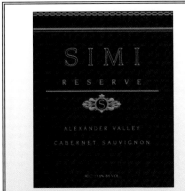

Simi Cabernet Sauvignon Reserve
has deep color intensity and rich fruit to complement the zesty lamb chop dish.

water to a boil in a small saucepan and blanch the lime skin for about 1 minute. Turn the heat down and add the sugar. Cook, simmering, for about 1 hour or until the liquid turns to a syrup. Remove from the heat and keep the syrup in a cool place. Reserve for later.

- Season the lamb chops with salt and pepper to taste. Fry the chops in a pan with the vegetable oil until browned on both sides. Set aside, keeping warm. Prepare the sauce.

- Deglaze the pan with the lamb stock, cooking over medium-high heat for about 2 minutes. Add the capers, olive paste, and the juice from the lime.

- To serve, cover the lamb chops with the sauce, placing 3 chops on each individual serving plate. Pour the lime syrup evenly over each chop, garnishing with the chives and chervil.

YIELD: 4 SERVINGS

Domaine de Valmouriane

Roasted Loin of Lamb Wrapped in Tapenade

Tapenade, the pastelike condiment that is strictly Provençal-born, coats the lamb as it cooks for the last part of its baking time. Tapenade is most commonly served with crudites or crackers and is derived from the Provençal word *tapeno*, meaning caper. Europeans eat lamb only very pink or not beyond an internal temperature of 140°. That is because pink lamb is very tender and gives off delicious juices. How you cook this recipe is a matter of personal preference, so adjust cooking times accordingly. Lamb is medium-rare at 145° and well-done at 165°.

TAPENADE:

½	cup black olives, pitted
1	ounce anchovies
1	ounce capers
2	tablespoons cognac

Roasted Loin of Lamb Wrapped in Tapenade and a strawberry tart at Domaine de Valmouriane

| ¼ | cup olive oil |
| ½ | cup unseasoned breadcrumbs |

LAMB:

4	pounds loin of lamb
	Salt and pepper
2	tablespoons butter
1	bulb garlic
½	cup white wine

ASSEMBLY:

| 2 | tablespoons butter |
| | Chicory for garnish |

🌿 🌿 🌿

- Preheat the oven to 350°. Season the lamb with the salt and pepper and place in a roasting pan. Place the lamb in the oven and cook for about 30 minutes, or until the lamb is just pink inside (more for desired doneness as described above.)
- Meanwhile, prepare the tapenade. In a blender, whirl together the olives, anchovies, capers, cognac, and olive oil, forming a purée. Remove the tapenade from the blender and mix in a bowl with the breadcrumbs. Set aside.
- In a small sauté pan, heat the butter and soften the chicory for about 5 minutes over medium heat.
- While the chicory wilts, remove the lamb from the oven. Place the unpeeled head of garlic in the roasting pan with the lamb. Then, cover the meat with the tapenade and return the pan to the oven to cook for another 10 minutes or until the tapenade is heated through.
- Remove the meat from the pan, discard the garlic, and deglaze the pan with the white wine. Allow the sauce to reduce. When the sauce has reduced, add the chicory.

YIELD: 4 TO 6 SERVINGS

Château de la Messardière

⌒𝖜𝖜⌒

The Saint-Tropez Ratatouille

Great as a side dish, this niçoise-version of ratatouille is served by Chef Jean-Louis Vosgien with a tartine tapenade or, in other words, a French baguette with an olive-paste spread. See page 187 for the tartine recipe.

¼	cup olive oil
8	ounces peeled eggplant, cut into ½-inch dice
8	ounces zucchini, cut into ½-inch dice
8-	ounce mixture red and green bell peppers, cut into ½-inch dice
½	cup finely chopped onion
2	large cloves garlic, finely chopped
8	ounces ripe, blanched, seeded, and skinned tomatoes, cut into ½-inch dice (about 2 medium tomatoes)
1	bay leaf
2	tablespoons fresh thyme, chopped
2	tablespoons fresh Italian parsley, chopped

- In a large skillet, heat the olive oil and sauté the eggplant, zucchini, peppers, onions, and garlic. Season with salt and pepper. Transfer to a medium stockpot and add the tomatoes, bay leaf, thyme, and parsley. Simmer, covered, over low heat for about 45 minutes to 1 hour. Uncover the pot and cook 15 minutes more to reduce the liquid, if necessary.

YIELD: 4 SERVINGS

Wine Suggestion

Château de Sancerre *is a crisp, dry white wine from the Loire Valley with the fruit and structure to stand up to any Provençal cuisine, including the Penne Primavera.*

La Bastide de Moustiers

Penne Primavera Provençal Style

½	**cup olive oil**
1	**teaspoon tomato purée**
½	**cup small fresh pearl onions, diced**
2	**small yellow onions, thinly sliced**
8	**ounces ripe tomatoes, blanched, skins and seeds removed, and tomatoes diced**
8	**ounces new potatoes, peeled and diced**
2	**cups penne pasta (fresh preferred), uncooked**
	Salt and pepper

The Penne Primavera Provençal style awaits guests in a delightfully secluded little dining room with just this one table at La Bastide de Moustiers.

1	clove garlic
8	sprigs fresh basil cut into a chiffonnade
½	cup chicken stock
½	cup grated Parmesan cheese

- Heat half of the olive oil in a medium saucepan. When the oil heats, add the tomato purée, pearl onions, yellow onions, tomatoes, and potatoes. Cook over medium-high heat until the vegetables brown. Add the penne. Season the mixture with salt and pepper. Add the garlic and basil. Turn the heat down to medium-low and slowly add the chicken stock. When the pasta has cooked *al dente*, sprinkle with the cheese and add the remaining olive oil. Serve while still warm.

YIELD: 4 SERVINGS

A cheese course is frequently served after meals and often finds its way into main dishes—such as this penne—as well.

La Bastide de Moustiers

Cherries and Almond-Vanilla Custard

Simple to prepare, this easy country-French dessert has overtones of the classic clafouti that originated in the Limousin region. The best-selling cherry varieties are Early Richmond, which debuts in the early spring, and English morello, a darker cherry that is available in late spring. Choose medium-firm cherries when buying the sour varieties.

2-3	cups sour fresh cherries such as Early Richmond or English morello, pitted
1	teaspoon vanilla extract
1¾	cups milk
½	cup powdered (finely ground) almonds
1	tablespoon cornstarch
½	cup sugar
3	eggs
	Confectioners' sugar

- Preheat the oven to 300°. Line a nonstick 8-inch round cake pan with the pitted cherries. Mix the vanilla with the milk and set aside.
- In a small bowl, mix together the almonds, cornstarch, sugar, and eggs. Add the milk mixture, stirring well to incorporate.
- Pour the batter over the cherries. Bake for 35 minutes or until golden.
- Sprinkle the top with the confectioners' sugar. Cut individual slices and serve while still warm.

YIELD: 4 SERVINGS

Royal Riviera

Chocolate Macaroons with Chocolate Sauce and Vanilla Yogurt

Almost brownielike in its texture and rich intensity, this dessert is uncomplicated and yet its effects are sophisticated and unusual.

MACAROONS:

8	ounces bittersweet chocolate
½	cup (1 stick) butter
6	eggs
½	cup sugar
2	tablespoons all-purpose flour
2	tablespoons or so clarified butter for greasing

CHOCOLATE SAUCE:

2	ounces semisweet chocolate
1	tablespoon heavy cream
1	tablespoon cocoa powder, plus more for garnish

GARNISH:

2	ounces vanilla yogurt
4	mint leaves
	Confectioners' sugar
	Vanilla ice cream, optional

- Preheat the oven to 375°. To prepare the macaroons, melt together the chocolate and the butter in a double boiler over medium heat. Set aside to cool. Meanwhile, whisk together the eggs and sugar in a medium bowl until pale yellow ribbons form. Sift the flour into the egg mixture and once the chocolate-and-butter mix-

The Chocolate Macaroons with Chocolate Sauce and Vanilla Yogurt are just as decadent and wonderful as a week spent at the Royal Riviera.

ture has cooled, stir it into the egg-and-flour mixture, blending with a spoon until well mixed.
- Coat 8 (2-inch) tart pans with the clarified butter. Fill each tart pan with approximately 2 ounces of the batter. Bake in the oven for 5 to 8 minutes or until soft but not crispy.
- Prepare the chocolate sauce. Melt the semisweet chocolate in a heavy-bottomed saucepan with the heavy cream and the cocoa powder. Stir the mixture and leave to melt. Once smooth and melted, strain the sauce through a sieve and set aside to cool slightly.
- To assemble, ladle 2 tablespoons of chocolate sauce onto an 8-inch dessert plate and place 2 of the macaroons in the center of the plate, slightly overlapping each other. Fill a small pastry bag (fitted with a small round tip) with the yogurt. Place tiny dollops of the yogurt on top of the chocolate sauce, all around the dish. Draw a toothpick through the dollops, creating a chained heart design. Garnish with a sprinkling of chocolate powder across the plate and a dash of confectioners' sugar, sprig of mint, and perhaps vanilla ice cream.

YIELD: 4 SERVINGS

Château de la Messardière

Glazed Chocolate Cake

CAKE:

½	pound good-quality dark chocolate
5	tablespoons butter
4	eggs, separated
¼	cup sugar
¼	cup all-purpose flour

GLAZE:

2	ounces quality milk chocolate
¼	cup heavy cream

- Preheat the oven to 350°.
- Melt the dark chocolate and the butter in a double boiler. Remove from the heat and let cool down.
- In a separate bowl, whip the egg yolks with the sugar and fold into the chocolate-butter mixture. Fold in the flour.
- In another bowl, whip the egg whites until stiff peaks form. Butter an 8-inch round baking pan. Fold the egg whites into the batter, and pour into the pan. Bake in the oven for about 20 minutes or until the cake sounds hollow when tapped. Allow the cake to cool down completely at room temperature before glazing.
- Make the glaze by melting the chocolate together with the cream in a double boiler. Set aside to cool. Glaze the cake and serve.

YIELD: 8 SERVINGS

The Glazed Chocolate Cake is just one of many sweet benefits of a stay here at the imposing Château de la Messardière in stylish St. Tropez.

The Hot Apple Tart comes straight out of the kitchen on a round iron peel for an eye-a-peel-ing presentation at La Bastide de Moustiers.

La Bastide de Moustiers

Hot Apple Tart

Lighter than an apple pie, this simple dessert is always a hit. Serve it with a cinnamon or pistachio ice cream, for added drama, add a little pastis, the national drink of Provence. With this apple tart recipe, you are making an applesauce that you spread over the pie shell before adding the sliced apples. It adds a delicious moist dimension to the tart.

PASTRY:

2¼	cups all-purpose flour
1½	cups (3 sticks) butter
1	cup sugar

½	teaspoon salt
1	egg

FILLING:

10	cooking apples, such as Granny Smith, peeled and cored
¾	cup sugar
½	cup firmly packed light brown sugar

- Preheat the oven to 450°. Mix together the flour, butter, sugar, salt, and the egg to form a dough. Knead the dough into a ball. Roll the dough out to ¼-inch thickness. Place in a 12-inch tart pan. (Note: if the dough is too tender, place it in the tart pan in pieces.)
- Bake the pastry in the oven for about 8 minutes or until golden. (Note: Do not brown the pastry.)
- Chop 4 of the apples coarsely. Place the apples in a sauté pan with the ¾ cup sugar. Sauté for 5 to 8 minutes or until soft. Set aside to cool.
- Remove the pastry from the oven. Turn the oven down to 350°. Cut the remaining apples into

¼-inch slices and set aside. Spread the applesauce evenly over the cooked tart dough. Then arrange the sliced apples on top in a circular fashion. Once the slices are on the tart, sprinkle with the brown sugar.

- Bake for another 10 or 15 minutes or until the apples caramelize and are cooked through. Remove the tart from the oven.

YIELD: 8 TO 10 SERVINGS

Château de la Messardière

Sautéed Banana Bundles with Pineapple-and-Rum-Cinnamon Sauce

CANDIED PEEL:

	Rind of 1 orange, cut julienne
½	cup water
¼	cup sugar

BANANA BUNDLES:

4	medium bananas
3	tablespoons clarified butter
12	phyllo dough sheets (cut 2 x 8 inches)
1	small bunch fresh mint

SAUCE:

½	fresh pineapple, peeled and cut into bite-size pieces
¼	cup plus 1 tablespoon sugar
1	vanilla bean
1	teaspoon ground cinnamon
2	tablespoons dark rum

- Make candied peel out of the orange rind. Blanch the julienne skins of the orange for 1 minute. Remove the peel from the water and mix it with the ½ cup water and ¼ cup sugar in a small saucepan. Cook over low heat for about 1 to 1½ hours or until most of the liquid has evaporated.
- Peel and cut each banana into 3 even pieces and pan-fry in 1 tablespoon of the clarified butter. Stack 3 phyllo sheets and brush with 1 tablespoon of the clarified butter. Roll the dough around the banana mixture and sprinkle with mint. In a large skillet, add the remaining clarified butter and pan-fry the wrapped banana bundles until they turn golden.
- In a medium saucepan, cook the pineapple pieces over medium-low heat with the sugar, vanilla, cinnamon, candied orange pieces, and the rum. Cook for 10 to 15 minutes or until tender. Remove the vanilla bean. Purée the fruit in a blender until smooth.
- To serve, arrange the banana bundles onto individual serving plates. Pour the pineapple-cinnamon sauce over them and decorate with more mint.

YIELD: 4 SERVINGS

BORDEAUX AREA AND THE ATLANTIC COAST

※ ※ ※

Vintage Wine, Pearl Oysters, and Golden Cognac

A sea of château-studded vineyards encircles Bordeaux, an elegant area rich in history and style. Bordeaux wines have been pleasing palates since the sixteenth century when Henry II, future king of England, married Eleanor of Aquitane. Henry encouraged local growers to produce wines on a large scale, increasing the area's trading position in Europe.

Today, wines are still the essence of life in this area, where sophisticated cuisine, also rooted in the vine, literally made a name for itself: *à la bordelaise.* Sauce *bordelaise* is one of Bordeaux's culinary best. The foie gras recipe with the spiced wine sauce in this section is a modern *bordelaise* interpretation. Foie gras and truffles are two of the area's prized culinary treasures.

The region includes the Alantic coast of France, so what better way to enjoy a glass of world-renowned wine than with a platter of oysters, caught off nearby shores?

Cognac: The Region and the Spirit

Cognac, named after the town in the Charente department in southwestern France, has been recognized for centuries as the finest region in the world for the production of grape-based spirits. This superb brandy became so closely associated with the region, that this fine and elegant spirit took the name of the town.

Cognac is made primarily from Ugni Blanc grapes, grown in legally defined areas that have unique chalk soils and microclimates. Districts such as Grande Champagne, Petite Champagne, Borderies, and Fins Bois are responsible for yielding grapes with intensity and balance. The cognac districts with the name *Champagne* (literally "fields") are not to be confused with the Champagne region in northeastern France, where sparkling wines are made.

To be known as cognac, the *eaux de vie* (water of life), which has been distilled twice in traditional copper-pot stills, must be aged in oak casks for years until it develops the rich and complex qualities of this spirit. While aging in a cask, about 2 to 3 percent of the volume is lost each year via evaporation, amounting to the equivalent of twenty million bottles. The loss is called *la part des anges,* or the angels' share. Before bottling, all cognac must be blended, using *eaux de vie* from different districts and different years.

There are recipes in this section that will tempt you to cook with cognac and experience the region's gastronomical claims to fame.

The chateau in Nieul, near La Chappelle St. Martin

Baked Mushroom Tart

Truffles make their way into many recipes in this region because they grow plentifully. This is a delicious mushroom recipe that you may season as desired. It is very simple to make and serves well as an appetizer.

½	cup olive oil
4	ceps or other boletus mushrooms, stems and caps separated
	Salt and pepper
4	ounces each, button and oyster mushrooms, chopped into small cubes
1	pound trumpet mushrooms (chanterelles), chopped into small cubes
⅔	cup butter
3	tablespoons chopped garlic
½	cup chopped shallots
2	tablespoons all-purpose flour
¼	cup Noilly Prat vermouth
½	cup heavy cream
¼	cup chopped flat-leaf parsley
2	eggs, beaten
1	cup beef marrow, poached and cut into slivers, optional
½	cup veal stock
¼	cup truffle juice
2	black truffles for garnish
1	small bunch chives for garnish

- Preheat the oven to 350°. Heat 2 tablespoons of the olive oil in a small sauté pan until hot. Sauté the heads and stalks of the ceps. Season with salt and pepper. Remove from the skillet with a slotted spoon. Line 4 (3½-inch) nonstick baking tins with the mushrooms. Set the tins aside.

- Heat the remaining olive oil in a medium sauté pan and add the garlic, shallots, and flour when the oil is hot. Cook until the vegetables sweat and just start turning golden brown. Season with salt and pepper. Deglaze the pan with Noilly Prat and keep stirring for 1 minute. Add the cream and cook a few minutes or until the cream is heated through and the sauce is smooth. Set the sauce aside to cool.

- When the sauce has cooled, add the parsley and the beaten eggs, mixing well to incorporate. Pour the mixture into the tins, dividing evenly. Add the slices of beef marrow (optional) and bake for 15 minutes or until the tart turns golden brown and a tester inserted comes out clean.

- Meanwhile, mix together the veal stock and truffle juice. Heat in a small saucepan. When the tarts are ready, turn them out onto a serving plate and decorate with the black truffles and chives. Servce with the sauce.

YIELD: 4 SERVINGS

Wine Suggestion

The Baked Mushroom Tart calls for the well-balanced richness of a champagne such as **Moët & Chandon White Star.**

The complex Pinot Noir, Pinot Meunier, and Chardonnay grapes found in this wine create a sense of harmony and refinement.

Le Moulin de l'Abbaye Restaurant, with its charming waterwheel and priceless views along the canal in the village of Brantôme

La Chappelle St. Martin

Pumpkin-and-Coconut Soup with Saffron

2	cups milk
¾	cup unsweetened shredded coconut
¼	cup olive oil
2	medium onions, finely chopped
8	ounces pumpkin or winter squash, peeled, and shredded
	Salt and pepper
2	threads saffron
2	cups light cream
	Chicken broth or stock (in case soup needs thinning)
4	celery leaves

- In a medium nonstick saucepan, bring the milk and coconut to a boil over medium-high heat. Boil gently on lower heat for 2 minutes. Remove from the heat and set aside.
- Heat the olive oil in a medium skillet and gently sauté the onions on medium heat until they turn translucent, about 3 minutes. Add the pumpkin to the onions and stir constantly for about 5 minutes; add salt and pepper to taste, then the saffron. Cook the mixture until a purée forms. Add the coconut milk and the cream. (Note: If the mixture is too thick, slowly add a little chicken stock or broth.)
- Remove the mixture from the heat and let cool down for about 10 minutes. Pour into a food processor and whirl until smooth. (You do not want a runny soup, but a thicker, smooth consistency.)
- Pass the mixture through a fine-mesh sieve. Season with salt and pepper. Garnish with chopped celery leaves.

YIELD: 4 TO 6 SERVINGS

½	teaspoon chopped chives

- Begin by making the sauce. Chop the tomatoes in a blender with the 2 ice cubes, the lemon juice, and olive oil. Preheat the oven to 400°. Slice the eggplant and zucchini lengthwise into ½-inch pieces. Place the eggplant and zucchini slices on a baking sheet and brush the tops with olive oil. Bake in the oven for 15 minutes or until just golden.
- In a small saucepan, steam the carrots until tender. Cook the green beans in water, about 6 minutes, and plunge in an ice bath to retain color. Cook the artichokes in water until tender. Remove and slice the artichokes into thin pieces.
- Line a terrine pan or 8-inch bread-loaf pan with plastic wrap, generously overlapping the edges. Place the zucchini, width-wise, lining the loaf of the pan with edges overlapping.
- Layer the remaining vegetables (ending with the zucchini on top), alternating varieties by layer.

The Vegetable Terrine with Tomato-Lemon Sauce at La Chappelle St. Martin in Nieul

La Chappelle St. Martin

Vegetable Terrine with Tomato-Lemon Sauce

SAUCE:

2	tomatoes, peeled, seeded, and cut in half
2	ice cubes
	Juice of ½ lemon
1	tablespoon olive oil

TERRINE:

10	ounces eggplant
8	ounces zucchini
2	teaspoons olive oil, or more for brushing
4	ounces green beans
2	medium carrots, cut into ½-inch pieces
2	artichokes, cleaned and tough top leaves cut back
2	medium tomatoes, peeled, seeded, and cut in half
	Salt and pepper

Wine Suggestion

The beautifully balanced Moët & Chandon Brut Impérial marries perfectly with vegetables, and lends that special touch to this terrine.

Brush each layer with olive oil and season with salt and pepper and a touch of cayenne.

- Place an identical loaf pan on top of the vegetables and add beans or heavy cans to weight down the vegetables. Refrigerate, covered with the plastic wrap, for 12 hours. Unmold and cut into ¾-inch slices.
- To serve, pool a small ladleful of sauce in the center of each individual serving plate. Slice 1-inch-thick pieces of the terrine and add 2 to each plate. Garnish with a sprinkling of chopped chives.

YIELD: 6 TO 8 SERVINGS

Château de Bagnolet

Bell-Pepper Custard with Tomato-Vinaigrette Dressing

CUSTARD:

1	tablespoon olive oil
2	green bell peppers, seeded and diced
2	red bell peppers, seeded and diced
2	onions, diced
2	tablespoons sugar
½	cup water
2	eggs
1	egg yolk
1¼	cups heavy cream
	Salt and pepper

DRESSING:

2	medium red ripe tomatoes, seeded
	Salt and pepper
2	tablespoons extra virgin olive oil
¼	cup red wine vinegar
	Fresh basil for garnish

- Preheat the oven to 350°. In a medium skillet, heat the olive oil and sauté the peppers and onions until lightly browned. Add the sugar and the water and cook over medium-high heat, about 8 to 12 minutes, or until the liquid evaporates. Transfer vegetables to a blender or food processor and coarsely grind them, along with the eggs, the yolk, the heavy cream, and a sprinkling of salt and pepper.
- Pour the mixture into 6 (3-inch) buttered ramekins and bake for 30 minutes or until set and just turning golden brown. Allow the custard to cool.
- Meanwhile, prepare the dressing. Finely chop the tomatoes, adding salt and pepper to taste. Add the olive oil and vinegar. Mix well.
- To serve, unmold the cooled custard and drizzle with the dressing. Add basil leaves for garnish.

YIELD: 6 SERVINGS

Wine Suggestion

The elegant Moët & Chandon Vintage Rosé has a creamy texture and the necessary complexity to enhance the flavors of the Bell Pepper Custard with Tomato Vinaigrette Dressing.

Château de Bagnolet

Sardines and Cognac Pâté

8	sardines
½	cup good-quality Cognac
½	cup (1 stick) butter
	Salt and pepper
1	tablespoon chopped chives

● Preheat the oven to 300°. Bake the fish for 5 to 7 minutes, or until heated through. Remove them from the oven and add to a skillet. Heat the skillet and flambé the fish with the Cognac. Season with salt and pepper. Remove the sardines from the skillet and let cool down. Crush the fish with a fork and mix with the butter, forming a paste. Mix in the chives and season again if desired. Serve with a crusty country French bread.

YIELD: 1 CUP PÂTÉ

Brantôme is a picturebook abbey town of canals, bridges, and medieval buildings—especially when viewed from an outdoor table of Foie Gras on Puff Pastry at Le Moulin de l'Abbaye Restaurant.

Le Moulin de l'Abbaye

Foie Gras on Puff Pastry with Fresh Figs and Spiced Bordeaux Wine Sauce

FIGS:

8	fresh good-quality figs, peeled and cut into thin slices
¼	cup raw sugar (sometimes called "turbinado" or "blond" sugar)

SAUCE:

1	tablespoon pure honey
2	teaspoons grated fresh ginger
3	black peppercorns
1	teaspoon juniper berries
1	whole clove
½	stick cinnamon
½	vanilla pod, or 1 teaspoon vanilla extract
	Peel of 1 orange
¼	cup quality wine vinegar, such as balsamic
2	cups medium-red Bordeaux wine
½	cup (1 stick) butter

FOIE GRAS:

1	tablespoon butter
4	8-ounce foie gras filets
4	2½-inch rounds cooked puff pastry
½	cup red currants

- Preheat the oven to 400°. Butter 4 (2½-inch) nonstick tartlet pans and sprinkle with the raw sugar. Place the fig slices in a circle around the tins and bake for about 8 minutes or until tender.
- In a small saucepan, heat the honey. Add the ginger, peppercorns, juniper berries, the clove, the cinnamon, vanilla pod, and orange peel and cook over medium heat until caramelized. Deglaze the pan with the vinegar and cook over high heat, reducing by half. Add the wine and reduce again by two-thirds. Pass the caramelized mixture through a sieve. Return to the stove and beat in the butter, heating until the butter is fully incorporated.
- In a large skillet, heat 1 tablespoon butter and sauté the foie gras filets until golden brown.
- Remove the figs from the baking tins and place on the pastry rounds. Arrange these on a serving dish with the red currants. Place the foie gras on top and lightly coat with the sauce.

YIELD: 4 SERVINGS

Château de Bagnolet

Warm Prawns and Summer Squash Salad with Raspberry Vinaigrette

Adjust the ingredient amounts here according to the number of persons you are serving. The salad is simple and refreshing and a nice change of pace.

1	large ripe tomato
½	medium summer squash
3	tablespoons olive oil, plus more for sprinkling
8	prawns or large shrimp, shelled and deveined
1	tablespoon raspberry vinegar
	Salt and freshly ground pepper
2	sprigs chervil or flat-leaf parsley, chopped, for garnish

* Cut the tomato into small wedges and remove the seeds; then dice. Do the same with the summer squash.
* Heat 2 tablespoons of the olive oil in a medium skillet and sauté the tomato and squash over medium heat until translucent. Remove from the heat and drain on a paper towel.
* Using the same skillet, heat the remaining tablespoon of the olive oil and sauté the shrimp for about 6 minutes, or until lightly browned. Drain on a paper towel.
* In a medium salad bowl, add the tomatoes, squash, and prawns. Add a sprinkling of olive oil and the vinegar, adding more if desired. Season with salt and pepper. Sprinkle with chopped chervil.

YIELD: 1 SERVING

Wine Suggestion

WHITE STAR

MOËT & CHANDON
CHAMPAGNE
APPELLATION D'ORIGINE CONTROLEE

ÉPERNAY ★ FRANCE

This well-balanced champagne has the intensity of flavor that is required for a variety of tastes and textures such as those found in this warm prawn salad.

Château de Bagnolet

Fruit Salad with Cognac Syrup

1	cup water
1	scant cup sugar
½	cup good-quality Cognac
3	bananas, sliced into thin rounds
½	pineapple, cut into thin triangular pieces
4	oranges, skins and seeds removed, and sliced in rounds, then cut in half
1	cup strawberries, quartered
1	cup seedless red grapes, removed from the vine
1	kiwi, peeled and cut into thin slices

* Prepare a simple syrup with the water and the sugar by bringing the 2 ingredients to a boil in a small saucepan over medium-high heat. Bring

the mixture just to a boil, then remove from the heat and stir in the Cognac. Allow the syrup to cool down.

- Arrange all of the fruits in a bowl, except for the kiwi. Pour the syrup into the bowl and stir

to combine and coat the fruits.

- Serve in individual bowls, garnished with slivers of kiwi.

———————

YIELD: 4 SERVINGS

Cognac, the finest of all brandies, is often enjoyed with dessert. It can also be used in the cooking process—such as here with these crêpes that were flamed with cognac and cherries.

Wine Suggestion

The subtle wood and honey flavors of Hennessy V.S.O.P Privilège— originally blended for the British royal family in 1817—perfectly complement the Beef and Bell Peppers in a Cognac Cream Sauce.

- Crush the peppers and rub them into the tenderloin. Sprinkle both sides of the meat with salt. In a skillet, heat the oil and quickly sear the beef on both sides, leaving it medium-rare inside. Remove the meat from the pan but keep it warm.
- Drain the pan of any grease and reuse the pan, setting it over medium-high heat. Deglaze the pan of meat bits with the Cognac. Add the veal stock and turn the heat down to a simmer, cooking until it reduces by half. Add the cream and reduce again, adding salt to season.
- Plate the beef and drape with the Cognac sauce. Serve with seasonal vegetables.

YIELD: 1 SERVINGS

Château de Bagnolet

Beef and Bell Peppers in a Cognac Cream Sauce

1	tablespoon finely diced green bell pepper
1	tablespoon finely diced red bell pepper
1	6-ounce beef tenderloin
	Salt
1	teaspoon vegetable oil
2	tablespoons good-quality Cognac
¾	cup veal stock
2	tablespoons heavy cream

Le Moulin de l'Abbaye

Prune Purée with Brandied Sabayon Sauce on Hazelnut Biscuits

Splendid ingredients create the essence of this gourmet-French dessert. The dessert is a crisp biscuit made with hazelnuts, topped with a purée of fruit and a classic cream sauce. The prunes and the cream pastry made with Armagnac—a fine French brandy, produced in the west, near Bordeaux—supply natural sweetness. A whisper of orange peel, cinnamon, and tea spice up the prunes.

BISCUIT:

½	cup (1 stick) butter
¼	cup sugar
½	cup ground hazelnuts

Fresh nuts of every variety can be found in local markets and are delicious in this recipe.

PRUNE PURÉE:

24	prunes, pitted
½	cup sugar
½	cup Armagnac or other good-quality brandy
1	teabag orange pekoe tea
1	teaspoon orange peel, plus more for garnish
½	teaspoon ground cinnamon

SABAYON SAUCE:

¼	cup sugar
½	cup water
2	egg yolks
½	cup whipped cream

ASSEMBLY:

	Mint leaves for garnish

- Preheat the oven to 350°. In a medium bowl, cream together the butter and sugar until smooth and well mixed. Add the hazelnuts. Pour the mixture into buttered 4-inch metal baking rings. Bake for 5 to 8 minutes or until lightly golden. Set aside.

- In a small saucepan, start the prune purée by poaching the prunes in just enough water to cover (about ¾ cup) with the sugar, brandy, teabag, orange peel, and cinnamon. (Note: You may opt to place the teabag in cheesecloth to ensure that it does not break during the cooking process.) When the prunes are hydrated and plump, remove 4 of them with a little bit of the cooking liquid and set aside to use as a garnish later.

- Prepare the sabayon sauce by first combining the ¼ cup of sugar with the ½ cup water and bring to a boil to make a simple syrup. Remove from the heat when the sugar is dissolved. Allow to cool completely. When the syrup has cooled, lightly beat in the egg yolks. Set the pan over low heat and beat continuously until you have a smooth, rich mousse. Cool the mixture and then fold in the whipped cream.

- Place the poached prunes on the 4 biscuits, evenly dividing the fruit. Evenly divide the sabayon sauce over prunes. Surround with the prune purée and decorate with mint leaves and more orange peel. Top each biscuit with the reserved prunes.

YIELD: 4 SERVINGS

Le Moulin de l'Abbaye

Chocolate Cherry Tarts

More like a brownie than anything else, this wonderfully soft cakelike dessert is easy to make and splendid-tasting. Morellos are dark mahogany-red, sour English cherries that are softer than sweet cherries. Choose morellos that are medium to firm, if buying them fresh. This recipe calls for the canned variety. At l'Abbaye, they serve this sweet with cherry sorbet.

½	cup (1 stick) butter
4	ounces quality semisweet chocolate
2	eggs
½	cup sugar
½	cup all-purpose flour
½	teaspoon baking powder
1	tablespoon cocoa powder
32	morello cherries, juice drained

ASSEMBLY:

	Confectioners' sugar for garnish
	Mint leaves for garnish

- Preheat the oven to 400°. In a double boiler, melt together the butter and chocolate. In a bowl, cream together the eggs and sugar and add this mixture to the melted chocolate, mixing well. Mix in the flour, baking powder, and cocoa. Pour the mixture into 4 (3½-inch diameter) greased pastry tart pans that are about ½-inch deep. Sink 8 cherries into each pan. Bake for 10 minutes or until set.
- Garnish with a dollop of sorbet if desired, or just dust with confectioners' sugar and garnish with a sprig of mint.

YIELD: 4 SERVINGS

Wine Suggestion

Moët & Chandon Demi-Sec is ideal for this chocolate-cherry combo, as it can be served with virtually any type of fruit dessert and is often used to bathe a fruit cocktail.

La Chappelle St. Martin

Coconut Custard with Strawberry-and-Lemon Sauce

CUSTARD:

	Butter
2	eggs
1	egg yolk
1	cup sweetened condensed milk
2	cups whole milk
1	teaspoon vanilla extract
¾	cup shredded unsweetened coconut

SAUCE:

1	cup strawberries, plus more for garnish
¼	cup confectioners' sugar
	Juice of ½ lemon
	Mint leaves for garnish

- Preheat the oven to 350°. Butter 4 to 6 (3- to 3½-inch) ramekins or custard cups. Place the cups in the refrigerator.
- In a medium bowl, beat the eggs and yolk until frothy. Beat in the condensed milk, the whole milk, and vanilla extract. Fold in the coconut. Remove the ramekins from the refrigerator and butter them again. Fill with the custard mixture. Place the custard cups in a warm bath (bain-marie), filled with water two-thirds the height of the ramekins. Bake for 25 minutes or until the

The Coconut Custard with Strawberry-and-Lemon Sauce

custard is set and golden brown. Remove from the oven and let cool at room temperature.
- Meanwhile, prepare the sauce. Purée the strawberries in a food processor with the sugar. Add the lemon juice and sugar and pulse quickly until incorporated. Taste the sauce and adjust seasoning, adding more sugar if necessary.
- To serve, place a pool of the sauce onto an individual dessert plate. Carefully unmold the custard onto the sauce. Decorate with strawberries and mint leaves.

YIELD: 4 TO 6 SERVINGS

Wine Suggestion

Rich texture and complex flavors of orange and spice characterize this luscious liqueur, which is perfect with the Coconut Custard with Strawberry-and-Lemon Sauce.

BRITTANY

※ ※ ※

Folksy Villages, Roadside Crêperies, and Apple Cider

Wild, wet, and windswept, Brittany's jagged, rocky coast surrounds a region practically untouched by the passage of time. Grassy meadows divide isolated villages and maritime towns, where Brittany's inhabitants developed culinary traditions as unique as the people themselves.

Bretons are believers in ritual and legend. Ancient tales include King Arthur and Merlin. Even the customary dress and language reflect their sense of history and individualism. Women wear tall lace headdresses, called *coiffes*, and men don classic wide-rimmed black hats.

Roadside crêperies or *galette maisons* sell thin pancakes filled with savory and sweet stuffings. Made with buckwheat flour, these flavorful creations are washed down with cups of golden cider. Brittany produces some of the world's best cider.

With the Atlantic Ocean as its backyard, Brittany's towns and villages have access to fresh seafood, with which they make the region's most famous dish, cotri-

ade, similar to bouillabaisse. Shrimp, lobster, and crayfish are in abundance as well as scallops, mackerel, mullet, sardines, tuna, and sea bass.

The uncomplicated nature of Brittany's cuisine calls for the much-needed addition of seasonings, especially salt. Salt is the region's most valuable trading commodity and was crucial to food preservation in the Middle Ages. Salt is still harvested in some areas of Brittany, in the ancient manner of hand-raking it out of shallow beds, and then selling it at roadside stands. Breton products that include salt are caramels, brioches, and specialty poundcakes.

Curry is a surprisingly common ingredient in Brittany. In the 1500s, the region gained a reputation for high-quality seafood, meat, and salted butter, bringing Mediterranean and Indian traders with oranges, dried fruits, and spices. Curry became so popular that the pungent spice ultimately made its way into traditional recipes.

Desserts satisfy the sweet tooth with the likes of butter cookies, sweet crêpes, and poundcakes. The Breton formula for notable cuisine is simplicity garnished with uncomplicated sauces and fresh, local products. It could not be more memorable.

The Lobster and Seafood Medley atop the nets at Audierne's fishing port, just outside Le Goyen's restaurant. (See recipe on page 170.)

Le Goyen

Oyster Velouté

Cockles are more popular in Europe than in the United States, for instance. They have a tendency to be quite gritty, so they must be cleaned well. If they are unavailable in your neighborhood, substitute with more oysters.

8	oysters
¼	cup unsalted butter
12	ounces cockles
½	cup chopped shallots
1	leek, white part only, shredded (discard the green part)
	Salt and pepper
⅓	cup white wine
1½	cups heavy cream
3	egg yolks
1	small bunch chervil

- Open the oyster shells and collect the juices. Pass the juices through a sieve to remove any particles. Reserve the juice.
- In a medium saucepan, heat half of the butter. Add the cockles and fry until the shells open, about 6 to 8 minutes. Remove the cockles from the pan and extract from the shells. Set aside. Reserve the juice from the pan.
- Heat the remaining butter in a skillet. Add the shallots and leeks, and season with salt and pepper. Sauté until the vegetables become translucent, about 8 minutes. Add the cockles and their juice. Stir in the oyster juice. Add about a third of the wine and cook for 6 to 7 minutes over medium heat. Add 1 cup of the heavy cream and cook for another 10 minutes. At about the 8-minute mark, add the oysters to fla-

vor the mixture and cook for the remaining 2 minutes.
- In a mixing bowl beat the egg yolks with the remaining ½ cup cream. Beat just until well blended. Set aside.
- Pass the seafood and wine mixture through a sieve and then into the bowl with the egg-yolk-and-cream mixture. Pour into a medium saucepan and cook over low heat until creamy.
- Pour the warm velouté or soup into bowls and garnish with chervil.

————

YIELD: 4 SERVINGS

Breton Crêpes with Scallops and Beurre Rouge in Le Goyen's colorful restaurant.

Le Goyen

Breton Crêpes with Scallops and Beurre Rouge

For a classic Breton dish, try this at home. The crepes are easy to make and the beurre rouge or red butter, comprised of only tomatoes, butter, and cream, gives fabulous gourmet results.

1½	cups (3 sticks) unsalted butter
4	leeks, white parts shredded (green parts discarded)
1½	cups thinned buckwheat pancake batter
	Salt and white pepper
2	whole ripe tomatoes, blanched, cut in half and seeded
1	cup heavy cream
½	cup olive oil
24	bay scallops, cleaned
	Chives, optional

- In a medium saucepan, heat ½ cup of the butter over medium-high heat. When the butter has melted, add the leeks. Season the leeks with salt and pepper and cook for 10 minutes until very tender.
- Using a flat nonstick griddle, (or a crêpe maker) prepare 4 paper-thin (8-inch) buckwheat pancakes, cooking them until crusty. Set the pancakes aside.
- In a food processor or blender, purée the tomatoes until smooth but thick. Pour the tomato purée into a small saucepan and add the remaining 1 cup of butter slowly, stirring it into the tomatoes. Add the heavy cream to make a beurre rouge, stirring for a smooth consistency. Remove the tomato sauce from the heat and set aside in a warm place.
- Heat the olive oil in a large skillet and sauté the scallops quickly, just until tender and cooked. Season with salt and pepper while cooking.
- To assemble the dish, place a crêpe on each dish and spread a tablespoon of the sautéed leek around the center of the crêpe. From here, you may gather up the edges of the crêpe and shape like a small bundle (tie with chives), adding the scallops outside the purse and pouring the sauce over all. Another way is more traditional. After you spread the leek confit around the crêpe, add a few scallops and fold the crêpe over in half. Pour the sauce over the middle of the crêpe. Garnish with more scallops, evenly dividing a total of 6 scallops per serving.
- Place 6 scallops onto each plate, next to the pancake purse, and gently pour the beurre rouge around the dish.

YIELD: 4 SERVINGS

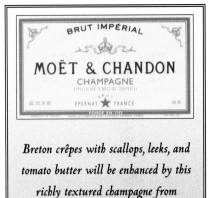

Le Goyen

Monkfish-and-Squid Pot with Armoricaine Sauce

In ancient times, Brittany was named Armorica, hence the name of the sauce for this dish. Well, maybe. Armoricaine sauce is made with shellfish, brandy, and wine, and it originated in Paris, not Brittany. Moreover, the addition of tomato, onion, and garlic came from a chef who created the sauce and he was from southern France.

The flinty Sauvignon Blanc grape makes Château de Sancerre a fine accompaniment to monkfish. Dry and flavorful, Sancerre is a classic match for all types of seafood.

The signs of crêpe-making are everywhere in Brittany.

All of this has nothing to do with Brittany and yet it is a popular sauce of this region.

Monkfish is a delicious fish that tastes rather like lobster for half the price. This is not difficult to prepare and is well worth the time.

FISH:

2	tablespoons olive oil
1¼	cups cleaned squid, cut into strips
2	pounds small white new potatoes, skins cleaned
	Salt and pepper
1¼	pounds mussels, cleaned
3	sprigs thyme

Germaine Bosser turns out tasty crêpes with great speed and agility in her quaint corner crêperie in Audierne.

1	bay leaf
2	tablespoons white wine
4	8-ounce monkfish filets, cut into bite-size pieces
2	large onions

SAUCE:

1½	cups butter
½	cup chopped carrots
1	cup diced onions
1	tablespoon each chopped thyme and parsley
4	pounds lobster shells, smashed into small bits
2	tablespoons tomato paste
½	cup all-purpose flour
1½	cups good-quality French brandy or Cognac

- In a large saucepan, heat the 2 tablespoons of olive oil. Add the squid strips and sauté over high heat until lightly browned, only a few minutes. Set aside.
- Boil the potatoes in salted water, cooking them for about 10 minutes or until tender. Drain and set aside. Keep warm.
- Place the mussels in a large pot with the thyme, bay leaf, and white wine, cooking the shellfish for 6 to 7 minutes or until the mussels open. Remove the bay leaf. Set the dish aside and prepare the sauce.
- Melt 1 cup of the butter in a large saucepan. Add the carrots, onions, garlic, and herbs and allow the vegetables to sweat for about 10 minutes over medium heat. Add the crushed lobster shells and keep sweating for another 10 minutes.
- Spoon in the flour and the tomato purée and stir well to incorporate.
- Deglaze the pan over high heat, flambéing with the brandy. Pour in the white wine. Cook the mixture for 15 minutes. Add about 4 cups of water. Bring the mixture to a boil and cook for 45 minutes longer, uncovered.
- Pass the mixture through a sieve, making sure the lobster shells remain behind. Season with salt and pepper.
- Add the monkfish and squid to a clean pan and add the Armoricaine sauce overtop. Cook for 7 to 8 minutes, warming the mixture thoroughly. Warm the mussels and potatoes.
- To serve, divide evenly among 4 soup bowls.

YIELD: 4 SERVINGS

Lobster-and-Seafood Medley on Potato Galettes with a Chive Cream Sauce

In Brittany potatoes and seafood flourish and this recipe exemplifies the region's finest.

2	lobsters, about 1 to 1¼ pounds each
½	cup (1 stick) butter
2	tablespoons peanut oil, plus more for frying
	Salt and pepper

GALETTE:

4	large white potatoes (about 8 ounces each), peeled and cut into very thin slices

LEEKS:

2	leeks, white part only
2	tablespoons butter

SAUCE:

2	tablespoons butter
1	small bunch fresh chives, finely chopped
¼	cup white wine
2	tablespoons heavy cream

ASSEMBLY:

12	cooked langoustines for garnish
16	sea scallops, sautéed in butter
2	pounds cooked (boiled) prawns or large shrimp
1½	cups button mushrooms, sliced

- Boil the lobsters for 5 minutes, then cook them in a large saucepan with ¼ cup of the butter and the 2 tablespoons of peanut oil. Season with salt and pepper. Cover the pan and cook over medium-high heat for 10 minutes. Set aside and keep warm.
- Heat the peanut oil in 4 (6-inch) frying pans (or cook 1 galette at a time) and then add the potato slices, arranging 1 sliced potato per pan, in a circle to form a pancake. Cook the potato pancakes or galettes over low heat, turning them on both sides and cooking until they are crispy. (Note: The starchiness of the potatoes seals the pancake together as it cooks.) Set aside and keep warm.

- Meanwhile, make a leek confit for garnish. Split the leeks in half lengthwise and then cut all halves into long slivers. Heat 2 tablespoons of butter in a skillet and sauté the leeks over low heat for about 10 minutes or until they are very soft. Set aside and keep warm.
- Return to the lobsters, removing them from the oil and cutting each of them in half lengthwise.
- Prepare the sauce by heating 2 tablespoons of butter in a saucepan. Add half of the chives and the white wine. Stir well and reduce just a couple of minutes. Add the cream. Season with salt and pepper. Transfer the sauce to a blender and whirl until completely smooth. Pass through a sieve and top with the remaining chives.
- To assemble the dish, place a potato galette onto each serving plate. Add half of a lobster, shell-side up. Divide the langoustines, scallops, prawns, and mushrooms among the 4 plates. Coat the lobster dishes with chive sauce and add the leeks. Serve immediately.

YIELD: 4 SERVINGS

Le Goyen

Frozen Grand Marnier Soufflé

4	egg yolks
¾	cup sugar
¼	cup Grand Marnier, plus more for soaking
1½	cups heavy cream
½	cup cubed candied orange peel
2	ladyfingers, sliced and soaked with Grand Marnier
	Raspberries for garnish
	Confectioners' sugar for garnish

- In a mixing bowl, beat the egg yolks with the sugar over a double boiler until thick and pale. Add the Grand Marnier and continue beating until the mixture is thick and frothy. Remove from heat and set aside.
- In another bowl, whip the heavy cream. Set aside.
- Line 4 greased (3½-inch) ramekins with parchment or waxed paper, allowing the paper to drop over the rim by 1 inch. Evenly divide the candied peel into each ramekin. Line the bottom of each ramekin with ladyfinger slices. Set aside.
- Pour the custard mixture into each ramekin and then add the whipped cream on top. Place each ramekin in the freezer for at least 4 hours or until frozen and ready to serve. Unmold each ramekin onto a serving plate. Garnish with fresh puréed raspberries and a dusting of powdered sugar.

YIELD: 4 SERVINGS

Le Goyen

Almond Mille-feuille with Strawberries and Cinnamon Cream

CRUST:

¾	cup ground almonds
¾	cup confectioners' sugar
1	tablespoon all-purpose flour
½	cup melted butter
2	tablespoons orange juice
2	teaspoons orange zest

SAUCE:

2	cups (1 pound) strawberries
1	tablespoon lemon juice

FILLING:

¾	cup heavy cream
½	cup pastry cream (see page 186)
1	teaspoon ground cinnamon
2	tablespoons sugar

GARNISH:

4	whole strawberries
	Mint leaves

Langoustines and a view of the water from Château de Locguenole along the Brittany coast

Étienne LeSquer takes a break from raking hay at a farm near Château de Locguenole in Brittany.

- Preheat the oven to 375°. Make the crusty layers of the mille-feuille with an almond paste. In a medium mixing bowl, mix together the almonds, confectioners' sugar, and the flour. Add the melted butter, the orange juice, and the zest. Work the mixture until smooth. Divide the paste into 12 equal (1-inch) balls (3 per person) and place them 2 inches apart on a greased baking sheet. Bake 15 minutes or until golden. Remove from the oven and let cool.
- While the crusts bake, prepare the strawberry sauce. Pour half of the fresh strawberries into a food processor and add the lemon juice. Purée until smooth. Set aside.
- Beat the heavy cream with 1 tablespoon or more of confectioners' sugar, if desired, to sweeten the cream. Beat until stiff peaks form. Fold the whipped cream into the pastry cream and stir in the cinnamon. Set aside. Slice the remaining whole strawberries, reserving 4.
- To serve, place a crusty disk on each of 4 serving plates. Pour a tablespoon of cinnamon cream onto each disk. Cover with sliced strawberries. Place another disk over the strawberries. Repeat, using another tablespoon of cinnamon cream and more sliced strawberries. End up with a third disk. Sprinkle with confectioners' sugar overtop. Garnish with a strawberry. Pool some of the strawberry sauce around the base of each mille-feuille. Garnish with a sprig of mint.

YIELD: 4 SERVINGS

NORMANDY

🌰 🌰 🌰

The Coming of Camembert and Calvados

Well-fed black and white cows grazing on lush grasses beneath groves of apple trees are a common sight almost anywhere in Normandy. This unusual combination explains a great deal about two distinct Norman culinary contributions—apples and cream—both making their presence known in the region's traditional menus.

The half-timbered, clay farmhouses on the rolling green pastures of Normandy are home to France's best-fed cows, producing some of the richest creams and cheeses in the world. Cream has been used liberally by Norman cooks for generations. Sauce Normande is the term here for simple French cream sauce.

With all of this dairy also come wagon-loads of cheese wheels and soft cheeses. Camembert is among the most popular cheeses produced all over the region by certain Norman cows. Unfortunately, as a result of widespread imitation of Camembert, the cheese must be stamped "appellation camembert controlée" to ensure authenticity. Other famous Norman

cheeses are Pont-l'Evêque and Livarot, found in the ravioli recipe in this section.

Interestingly, Camembert is made in Calvados, where another world-renowned product is made. Many recipes are prepared with, or accompanied by, the famous Calvados, a brandy made from the distillation of fermented apple juice. Originally employed as a medicine in the sixteenth century, Calvados is even enjoyed here for breakfast, or mixed with apple juice as an

Normandy is famous for its dairy products and Mont St. Michel, a spectacular island/church dating to the 11th century.

apéritif. The Norman diner carries out the ritual of *le trou normande,* pausing during the meal for a swallow from a glass of Calvados to aid digestion. Used as recipe ingredients, apples and Calvados contribute to the unique character of Norman cuisine. Eggs with apples and Calvados, crêpes stuffed with Calvados-soaked apples, and many varieties of apple tarts and sauces abound.

With its miles of sandy dunes and beaches, Normandy's coast has always had access to an abundance of seafood. Shellfish, sole, monkfish, turbot, and brill are only a few of the daily catches available.

Norman dishes are almost always served with breads that are as individual as the cuisine. Pain brie, for example, is a dense, rectangular white loaf—a perfect match for hearty soups and stews. With the staff of life, a few apple slices, a small carafe of Calvados, and some of that Camembert cheese, one can escape to Normandy at the nearest sandy beach. Meanwhile, these recipes will take you there vicariously in your kitchen.

Le Manoir du Lys

Foie Gras and Apple Salad with Calvados and Cider-Mustard Vinaigrette

Two of Normandy's local products—apples and Calvados—combine with France's famed foie gras and Dijon mustard to make a perfectly light and satisfying salad, including an apple cider vinaigrette. Chicken breast makes a nice substitute for the foie gras.

VINAIGRETTE:

2	shallots, minced
2	tablespoons Dijon mustard
	Salt and pepper
¼	cup olive oil
1	cup vegetable oil
⅓	cup apple cider vinegar

Dijon mustard, apples, Calvados, and foie gras are the key ingredients in this delightful salad.

APPLES:

4	Granny Smith apples, peeled, cored, and cut into sixths
	Juice of 1 lemon
1	cup water
½	cup (1 stick) or more butter
¼	cup Calvados

ASSEMBLY:

12	ounces foie gras, cut into ¼-inch pieces (3 per person)
2	tablespoons butter
4	cups or more variety of tender nonbitter leafy greens such as curly-leaf lettuce, Bibb or Boston lettuce, chicory, or mâche

- In a small bowl, stir the minced shallots with the mustard. Season with salt and a few grinds of pepper. Slowly drizzle most of the olive and vegetable oils into the mustard mixture, whisking vigorously. Whisk in the apple cider vinegar and the rest of the oils. Set the vinaigrette aside in the refrigerator until later.
- Tournée or cut the apple pieces into quenelle shapes. (This is optional.) Mix together the lemon juice and water and pour in a bowl over the apples. In a medium saucepan, melt the butter over medium heat and sauté the apples in the lemon water mixture until the liquid reduces and the apples are golden and still somewhat crunchy. You do not want the apples to overcook or become mushy. Add ¼ cup of the Calvados, turning up the heat. Flambé the apples and cook until the alcohol has dissipated. Remove the apples from the heat and set aside.
- To assemble the dish, season the foie gras with salt and pepper. In a medium skillet, melt the 2 tablespoons of butter and sauté the foie gras over medium-high flame 1½ to 2 minutes per side. Add the remaining Calvados and flambé.
- Toss the greens in the vinaigrette. Arrange on each serving plate with the foie gras on top and the apples around the edge. Serve immediately.

YIELD : 4 SERVINGS

Le Manoir du Lys

Foie Gras Soup

The chef at the manor usually offers this soup in demitasse cups, complements of the chef. It is a nice idea to have this rich, delicious soup waiting on a tray as your guests arrive.

9	ounces foie gras
2	eggs
	Salt and pepper
⅛	teaspoon grated nutmeg
½	cup heavy cream, heated
2	egg whites
1½	cups chicken stock
¼	cup truffle juice

- Press the foie gras through a sieve into a bowl and add the whole eggs and salt, pepper, and nutmeg. Pour the heated cream into the bowl and beat the mixture until smooth. Pour into a large double boiler and cook for 10 minutes. Remove from heat.
- Beat the egg whites and the chicken stock in a mixing bowl. Add salt and pepper to taste and the truffle juice. Pour the mixture into the foie gras mix and cook over the double boiler again for 8 minutes. Eat cold, lukewarm, or hot.

YIELD: 4 DEMITASSE-SIZE SERVINGS

Normandy's famous cheeses come together for this ravioli in the garden at Le Manoir du Lys.

RAVIOLI DOUGH:

1	cup all-purpose flour
	Salt
½	cup boiling water
1	tablespoon vegetable shortening

RAVIOLI FILLING:

2	carrots, finely diced
2	turnips, finely diced
2	zucchini, finely diced
	Salt and pepper
2	tablespoons butter
6	ounces Camembert cheese
6	ounces Livarot cheese
6	ounces Pont L'Evêque cheese

Le Manoir du Lys

Vegetable-and-Normandy-Cheese Ravioli with Calvados Sauce

Camembert, Livarot, and Pont-l'Evêque cheeses are typical of the Normandy area. Camembert is widely available in the United States and the two other cheeses may be found in specialty stores. Livarot is one of the earliest traditional Norman cheeses, made from cow's milk in the Calvados region. It has a smooth texture and a washed, brownish red rind. Pont l'Evêque has a strong taste and scent but a similar texture to the other two cheeses. This classic pasta dish from Normandy includes Norman products such as hard cider for which you may substitute another product of the region—Calvados or other apple brandy.

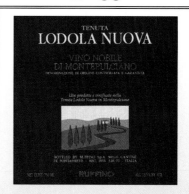

"Get a taste of Normandy at the farm," a Calvados farm in this case

SAUCE:

2	**shallots, minced**
1½	**cups hard cider**
½	**cup cider vinegar**
1½	**cups veal stock**
1½	**cups heavy cream**
2	**tablespoons butter**

- Make the dough for the ravioli. Place the flour, salt, boiling water, and vegetable shortening in a food processor and whirl for 3 minutes until smooth and a dough ball forms. Place dough in the refrigerator and make the ravioli stuffing.
- Boil the vegetables in water until tender. Drain. Season with salt and pepper and add the butter. Remove the rinds from the cheeses and melt the cheeses in a double boiler. Mix the vegetables into the cheese and set aside in the refrigerator.

- In a small saucepan, prepare the sauce. Sauté the shallots in the cider and vinegar. Reduce the sauce by half. Add the veal stock. Cook and reduce for another 3 minutes over medium-high heat. Add the cream and the butter and cook until incorporated. Keep warm.
- Spread the dough out with a rolling pin and put through the pasta machine, creating 2 (14-foot) lengths of dough. Remove the stuffing from the refrigerator. Place teaspoons of filling on 1 sheet of dough, about 1 inch apart. Cover with another sheet of dough. Cut the ravioli with a sharp knife. Pinch each ravioli around the edges to seal. Place in the refrigerator for 30 minutes.
- Steam the ravioli in a steamer. Serve 3 ravioli per person with the cider sauce.

YIELD: 24 RAVIOLI (8 SERVINGS)

Cream of Mushroom Soup

This is a classic mushroom soup that may be frozen in batches if you prefer fewer servings. For a variation, Le Manoir garnishes this soup with sautéed scallops

10	shallots, minced
½	cup (1 stick) butter
8	ounces chanterelle mushrooms, chopped
8	ounces ceps (porcini) mushrooms, chopped
8	ounces button mushrooms, chopped
4	cups chicken stock
4	cups heavy cream

- Lightly sauté the shallots in the butter in a medium saucepan. Add the mushrooms and brown in the butter. When the mushrooms have browned, deglaze the pan with the chicken stock. Allow the mixture to simmer on low heat for 20 minutes. Add the cream and simmer another 20 minutes. Transfer the mixture to a blender and purée until smooth. Season with salt and pepper.

YIELD: 10 SERVINGS

Quail with Mushrooms à la Grecque

½	cup olive oil
2	tablespoons minced onion
1	teaspoon ground coriander
	Salt and pepper
1½	cups white wine
2	tablespoons mixed chopped herbs
1½	pounds button mushrooms (tops only), coarsely chopped
¼	cup fresh lemon juice
¼	cup tomato juice
½	cup tomato purée
8	quail
	Chervil for garnish

- Heat the olive oil in a medium skillet. Sauté the onion and coriander with salt and pepper. Add the wine and the mixed herbs. Cook for 5 minutes. Add the mushrooms and the lemon juice. Cover and cook for 5 minutes. Remove the mushrooms and set them aside. Add the tomato juice, the tomato purée, and reduce for 10 minutes over medium-high heat. Return the mushrooms to the pan. Set aside.

Wine Suggestion

PRODUCE OF FRANCE — SANCERRE WHITE WINE

SANCERRE
APPELLATION SANCERRE CONTRÔLÉE

Château de Sancerre
Mise en bouteilles au Château par
MARNIER-LAPOSTOLLE · PROPRIETAIRE
18300 SANCERRE FRANCE

Alc 12.5 % by vol   CONTAINS SULFITES   contents 750 ml

The crisp fruit and flinty character of
Château de Sancerre, from France's
famed Loire Valley, will burst
through the creaminess of the
mushroom soup.

- Bone the quail. Remove the filets and cook them in a saucepan for 2 minutes on each side. Remove from the pan and do the same with the drumsticks.
- Evenly divide the mushroom mixture among individual serving dishes. Place the hot quail pieces (1 quail per person) on top. Garnish with chervil.

YIELD: 8 SERVINGS

*W*ine *Suggestion*

Cuvée Dom Pérignon Rosé

champagne—made from Pinot Noir and Chardonnay grapes—has lively, bright fresh fruit and an underlying richness that will enhance the flavors of the quail with mushrooms.

Spicy Poached Pears

	Sugar syrup made from 1 quart of water and 2 pounds of sugar
4	pears, peeled
	Juice of 4 lemons
2	tablespoons ground cinnamon
1	teaspoon ground ginger
1	teaspoon freshly ground nutmeg
4	bay leaves, optional
4	branches fresh thyme, optional
4	vanilla beans, optional

- Bring the syrup to a boil in a large saucepan. Stir in the cinnamon, ginger, and nutmeg. Add the pears and lemon juice. Slowly cook the pears until boiling and fork tender, about 10 minutes.
- Place 1 pear per person in a small bowl and add some of the syrup. (Reserve the remaining syrup for another recipe.) Decorate with a bay leaf, a sprig of thyme, and a vanilla pod, if desired. Serve lukewarm.

YIELD: 4 SERVINGS

PANTRY BASICS

Basic Pasta Dough

2⅓	cups all-purpose flour, plus more for dusting
½	teaspoon salt, optional
3	large eggs

- Add the flour and salt to a food processor and process briefly with the metal blade just to blend. Drop the eggs in through the feed tube, and let the machine run (about 1 minute) until a dough begins to form in the shape of a ball. If the dough is too sticky, add a tablespoon or more of flour. If it is too dry, add a few drops of water, or a few drops of beaten egg. Process again briefly.
- Turn the dough out onto a floured surface. Dust your hands with flour and knead for 3 to 5 minutes, adding more flour if necessary, until you have a smooth ball of dough. Set it to rest in a tea towel or plastic wrap for about 30 minutes.
- Roll the dough out and pass through a pasta machine several times to reach the desired thickness.

YIELD: 1 POUND PASTA DOUGH

The inviting beach and colorful Amalfi coast town of Atrani

Chicken Stock

2	pounds raw or cooked chicken meat and/or bones
2	quarts water
2	ribs celery, cut into 1-inch pieces
1	carrot, cut into 1-inch pieces
1	onion, cut in half
1	bay leaf
2-3	parsley stems
6	peppercorns
	Salt

- Place the chicken in the stockpot. Add the water, celery, carrot, onion, bay leaf, parsley, peppercorns, and salt to taste. (When salting the chicken stock, some of the liquid will evaporate and the stock will become more concentrated. Be careful not to oversalt). Bring to a boil and skim the scum as it rises. Reduce the heat and partially cover and simmer the stock for 1½ to 2 hours. Add more water if the liquid evaporates and the bones or vegetables are not covered.
- Strain the stock through a colander into a large bowl and cool it uncovered. Refrigerate the stock and remove the congealed fat from the surface. Store the stock in the refrigerator for several days or freeze it in smaller containers.

YIELD: 1½ QUARTS

Foie gras and fraises, *or strawberries, are good cause to make a quick stop along the road in rural France.*

In a medium stockpot, brown the beef bones. Add the vegetables and sweat them until they turn a golden brown. Remove any excess fat or oil. Add the tomato paste and cook for 5 minutes more. Add the wine and then the bay leaf and thyme. Add the water and bring back to a boil. Skim the surface and then turn down the heat to a simmer. Simmer gently for 2 hours then pass through a sieve.

YIELD: ABOUT 4 CUPS

Lamb Stock

This recipe, from Chef Jean-Louis Vosgien of Château de la Messardière, will keep for months in the freezer. You may also use this method to make a veal, chicken, or any other stock, just substitute for the lamb.

2	pounds lamb bones (with meat scraps)
2	carrots, coarsely diced
2	medium onions, coarsely diced
3	cloves garlic
1	bunch parsley
1	bay leaf
⅛	teaspoon thyme
4	ripe tomatoes, chopped
1	rib celery, chopped

Brown the lamb bones and scraps in a saucepan on the stovetop with the carrots and onions. Transfer to a large stockpot. Add the remaining ingredients and add enough water to cover. Simmer the stock for about 3 hours. Strain.

YIELD: 4 TO 6 CUPS

Beef Stock

2	pounds beef bones
	Salt and pepper
¼	cup chopped onion
2	tablespoons chopped carrot
2	tablespoons chopped leek
2	tablespoons chopped celery
2	tablespoons tomato paste
¾	cup red wine
1	bay leaf
1	tablespoon dried leaf thyme
4	cups cold water

Fish Stock

2-3	pounds fish bones or frames
2-3	quarts water
	Salt

- (If using whole fish frames, gut them, remove the gills, and wash them as well as the fish bones under cold running water. Cut them to fit in the stockpot.)
- Place the fish bones in a large, nonreactive stockpot. Add water to cover, about 2 to 3 quarts, and salt to taste. Bring to a boil and skim the scum as it rises. Reduce the heat, cover the pot, and simmer for about 20 minutes.
- Strain the stock through a colander, removing the bones. Cool, cover, and refrigerate or freeze until ready to use.

YIELD: 1½ QUARTS

Guards at the Vatican

Quick Brown Sauce

Be sure to check your requirements when making this for a specific recipe. You may have to increase the ingredients.

2	tablespoons butter
1	clove garlic, finely minced
2	tablespoons all-purpose flour
1	cup beef broth or bouillon
1	teaspoon dry sherry
1	teaspoon Worcestershire sauce
1	teaspoon lemon juice
1	tablespoon mixture of fresh herbs: rosemary, thyme, sage, basil
	Salt and pepper

- Melt the butter in a small saucepan over medium-high heat. Sauté the garlic but do not brown. Stir in the flour until blended. Pour in the broth and bring to a boil. Add the sherry, Worcestershire, lemon juice, and herbs. Season with salt and pepper. Cook for 2 minutes more and adjust seasonings as desired.

YIELD: 1 CUP

Crème Fraîche

Many recipes—from savories to sweets—call for crème fraîche. The cream is great for cooking in sauces and soups because it will not curdle. It is also delicious spooned over fresh fruits, fruit cobblers, or puddings. Crème fraîche is really a product of France, where the cream is not pasteurized and therefore contains the bacteria necessary to thicken it naturally. In countries such as the United States—where cream is pasteurized—the fermenting agents necessary to make this thick cream are not present. You can buy crème fraîche in specialty stores in many countries, including America, but it is very costly. The following alternative is a perfect substitute.

(Crème fraîche may be flavored with items such as minced garlic and herbs, horseradish, or honey.)

| 1 | cup whipping cream |
| 2 | tablespoons buttermilk |

- Combine the cream and buttermilk in a screw-top glass container. Cover and let stand at room temperature for 8 to 24 hours, or until the mixture becomes very thick. Stir well and replace lid. Place in the refrigerator for up to 10 days.

Squash blossoms—or the flowers of zucchini—are an edible flower and a popular ingredient throughout Italy and France. They are often stuffed with cheese or simply breaded and fried.

Pastry Cream

This is a basic recipe for filling pastries and an assortment of other desserts.

4	eggs
2	egg yolks
1¼	cups sugar
½	cup cornstarch
1	quart milk
1	tablespoon pure vanilla extract
2	ounces unsalted butter

- In a medium mixing bowl whisk together the eggs, egg yolks, and ½ cup of the sugar, mixing well. Add the cornstarch and whisk to remove any lumps. Set aside.
- In a heavy stainless steel saucepan, dissolve the remaining ¾ cup sugar in the milk and vanilla,

and bring just to a boil. Slowly pour half of the milk-and-vanilla mixture into the egg mixture, while whisking. (This brings the temperature of the egg mixture equal with the milk and prevents curdling.) Pour this mixture back into the saucepan with the other half of the milk and reduce the heat on the stove to low. Bring to a slow boil, stirring constantly to prevent burning and lumping. (At this stage the pastry cream will start to thicken rapidly and it is important that it be briskly stirred at all times.)

- The pastry cream should be thick and stick to the back of a spoon when done. Remove immediately from the stove and place into the bowl of a mixer with the paddle attachment.
- Add the butter and beat on medium speed until completely cooled. (This prevents the growth of bacteria and cools the cream quickly to stop the

cooking process.) Once cooled, place into a shallow container and cover with plastic wrap, directly touching the surface of the pastry cream. This prevents a tough outer skin from developing. Refrigerate for at least 2 hours before use.

YIELD: 1 QUART

⟍ᗢᗢᗢᗢᗢᘖ

Tapenade Tartines

Tartine in French means a baguette covered with a coat of jam or butter, or such savory spreads as tapenade. Here is a recipe that can be served as an appetizer or as an accompaniment to the recipe on page 143 for the Saint-Tropez Ratatouille. (Another nice variation of this recipe from Château de la Messardière is to spread the baguette with anchovies or anchovy paste instead of the tapenade or olive paste, and add some fresh basil on top.)

Baguettes
Olive oil
Tapenade or olive paste (see page 142)

🌿 🌿 🌿

- Cut the baguettes in ½-inch slices and grill in an oven or toaster oven until toasted. Sprinkle a few drops of the olive oil onto each baguette. Spread generously with the tapenade and serve.

Lemons brighten the entryway to a tiny grocery store in the village of Ravello.

Anchovies Stuffed with Mozzarella

Make as many or as few as you wish. From the Hotel Belvedere Caruso, this is fast and simple. Just filet 2 anchovies, stuff each one with a thin piece of Mozzarella cheese, and roll up jellyroll style. Place on a grill and cook until just browned. Serve immediately with freshly squeezed lemon juice.

Bruschetta with Goat Cheese and Red Peppers

My favorite cheese is goat cheese or chèvre and my favorite appetizer is bruschetta or crusty Italian bread slices brushed with olive oil and just about any topping. Serve this as an appetizer to an Italian entrée, or serve with a bowl of soup and salad, and call it a bistro dinner.

1½	pound loaf crusty Italian bread
2	tablespoons light olive oil, plus ½ teaspoon
4	ounces soft variety goat cheese, crumbled
2	ounces Neufchâtel cheese (light cream cheese)
2	teaspoons fresh lemon juice
1	teaspoon fresh snipped sage or oregano or
½	teaspoon dried sage or oregano
¼	cup coarsely chopped black olives
¾	cup freshly roasted red peppers, cut into thin strips
	Sage leaves for garnish

Polenta, ground at an old mill in the mountains of the Valle d'Aosta region

- Preheat the oven to 425°. Cut the bread into ½-inch-thick slices and lightly brush both sides with the 2 tablespoons of oil. Place the bread on a baking sheet and cook in the oven for about 10 minutes or until crisp and light brown, turning over each slice once. Let stand at room temperature while preparing the topping.
- In a medium bowl, stir together the cheeses, lemon juice, and herbs. Toss the olives with the ½ teaspoon olive oil.
- To assemble, spread each slice of bread with the cheese mixture. Add red pepper strips and the chopped olives. Garnish with fresh sage leaves. Serve warm or at room temperature. To heat, return the slices to the oven and bake for 3 minutes at the same cooking temperature.

YIELD: ABOUT 24 SERVINGS

Resource Directory

Berlitz International, Inc.
293 Wall Street
Princeton, NJ 08540
Phone: (609) 924-8500
*   (800) 257-9449*

Berlitz, the premier language services organization with 320 Language Centers in 33 countries, has been helping people communicate since 1878. Consumers as well as business people come to Berlitz to open new channels of communication through language instruction, cross-cultural training, and translation and interpretation services. The company also provides a wide-range of language- and travel-related publishing products. French and Italian instruction was provided to the staff of *World Class Cuisine* by Berlitz.

Ceramiche Rampini
Casa Beretone di Vistarenni
Radda in Chianti, Italy 53017
Phone: 39 577 73 80 43
Fax: 39 577 73 87 76

A family owned and operated business in the heart of Chianti country, producing ceramic pottery with uniquely individual designs and brilliant colors.

Grey Poupon Dijon Mustard
Nabisco Foods, Inc.
East Hanover, NJ 07936
Phone: (800) NABISCO (622-4726)

From sandwiches to gourmet main courses, any dish can be enhanced with the zesty flavor of Grey Poupon Mustards—Original Dijon, Spicy Brown, Country Dijon, Honey, Horseradish, and Peppercorn.

Maison du Cadeau
12 Rue du 14 Juillet
Cognac, France 16100
Phone: 33 45 82 05 62

Purveyor of fine Limogese china, not far from the city of Limoges, France, in the village of Cognac.

Schieffelin & Somerset Co.
Two Park Avenue
New York, NY 10016
Phone: (212) 251-8269
*   (800) 257-9449*

Schieffelin & Somerset paired wines with recipes throughout this book. The company is an importer for premium wines and spirits such as Moët & Chandon Champagne, Hennessy Cognac, Grand Marnier, Johnnie Walker Blended Scotch Whiskies, Tanqueray Gin, and Tanqueray Sterling Vodka.

Berlitz offers Individual Instruction (below), as well as Semi-Private and Small-Group.

Restaurant Directory

ITALY

Al Vecchio Convento Ristorante e Albergo
Via Roma, 7
Portico di Romagna
Italy
Phone: 39 543 967 752
Chef Giovanni Cameli

Located in the tranquil Emilia Romagna countryside, Al Vecchio Convento is a cozy Italian retreat. Tiled floors, wood ceilings and open hearth fireplaces are authentic reminders of the noble 19th-century home it once was.

Ristorante L'Arsenale
Via S. Giovanni a Mare, 20-262
Minori
Italy
Phone: 39 89 851 418
Chef Luigi Proto

An authentic Southern-Italian dining experience is what Ristorante L'Arsenale offers to visitors of the tiny fishing village of Minori. Blessed with wood burning ovens and a proximity to the sea, pizza and seafood dishes are the specialties of this traditional Campania restaurant.

Caruso Belvedere
Via Toro, 52
84010 Ravello
Italy
Phone: 39 89 857 111
Chef Giovanni Cioffi

Originally an 11th-century palace built for the Marquis D'Afflitto, the Hotel Caruso Belvedere still retains its regal features—Corinthian pillars, marble sculptures and extensive gardens represent a respect for Italian culture and tradition. Commanding views of the blue Amalfi coast only accentuate the villa's inherent beauty and serene atmosphere.

Castello di Spaltenna
53013 Gaiole in Chianti
Italy
Phone: 39 577 749 483
Chef Seamus de Pentheny O'Kelly

This ancient monastery captures the spirit of the natural Tuscan countryside. With stone walls, high-beamed wood ceilings and colorful hand-painted fabrics, Castello di Spaltenna is a luxurious yet comfortable sanctuary encircled by the famous Chianti vineyards.

Certosa di Maggiano
Strada di Certosa, 82
53100 Siena
Italy
Phone: 39 577 28 81 80
Chef Stefano Cosattini

Enveloped by vineyards and olive groves, Certosa di Maggiano remains true to its spiritual origins. Built as a Carthusian Monastery in 1314, the hotel provides a genuine medieval Tuscan atmosphere, tastefully combined with modern comforts.

At the entry to Castello di Spaltenna

Grand Hôtel Cocumella

Via Cocumella, 7
80065 Sorrento-Sant'Agnello
Italy
Phone: 39 81 878 29 33
Chef Rosa Russo

Resting on a rocky palisade on the edge of the Bay of Naples, Grand Hôtel Cocumella is a legendary cloister of peaceful gardens and spectacular views. Mount Vesuvius looms majestically across the bay, and tiny Mediterranean islands dot the clear blue sea as far as the eye can see.

Le Sirenuse

Via Cristoforo Colombo, 30
84017 Positano
Italy
Phone: 39 89 87 50 66

Built in the 18th century as a summer home for Italian nobility, this enchanting Positano villa is perched on a hillside overlooking the Amalfi Coast. Its magnetic charm is enhanced by a special feature: guest rooms face the sea.

Hôtel Lord Byron

Via G. De Notaris, 5
00197 Rome
Italy
Phone: 39 6 36 13 041
Chef Antonio Sciullo

The Hotel Lord Byron is a modern tribute to the spirited English author. Classic decor and elegant dining reflect a bygone era of romanticism and individuality.

Il Bottaccio

Via Bottaccio, 1
54038 Montignoso
Italy
Phone: 39 585 34 00 31
Chef Pina Mosca

Located within the walls of an 18th century olive press, this delightful inn and restaurant pays respect to the traditional Tuscan way of life. High-beamed ceilings and stone-paved floors frame original olive press equipment dispersed throughout this historic structure.

La Chiusa

Via della Madonnina, 88
53040 Montefollonico
Italy
Phone: 39 577 66 96 68
Chef Dania Lucherini

A view of Positano from Le Sirenuse (meaning The Sirens) resort

Wonderful aromas of freshly baked bread float through this classic Tuscan farmhouse any time of day. The restaurant's wood-burning oven is just a small example of La Chiusa's dedication to preserving an ambiance of rustic simplicity.

La Riserva di Castel d'Appio

18039 Ventimiglia
Italy
Phone: 39 184 22 95 33
Chef Franco Biamonti

One-thousand feet below La Riserva is the Mediterranean Sea. On a cliff high above the inn sit the ruins of an ancient Italian castle. From wherever you are in this Riviera dei Fiori inn, the views are grand and the cuisine first rate.

Le Grand Hôtel

Via V. E. Orlando 3
00185 Rome
Italy
Phone: 39 6 4709
Chef Paolo Moretti

Rome's renowned luxury hotel is more like an aristocratic palace. Located in the heart of Italy's great city, its grand salons and ornate reception rooms have hosted an impressive guest list of international dignitaries and noteworthy individuals.

Locanda dell' Amorosa

Localita Amorosa
53048 Sinalunga
Italy
Phone: 39 577 679 497
Chef Walter Redaelli

What was once a barn stall occupied by Tuscany's signature white cattle is now the rustic, yet refined restaurant of Locanda dell' Amorosa—a former medieval hamlet. While undergoing renovatins, great care was taken to respect the original design of ancient Tuscan structures.

Neiges d'Antan

Cret. 11021
Breuil-Cervinia
Italy
Phone: 39 166 948 775
Chef Luca Risso

Secluded in the majestic Italian Alps and facing the Matterhorn, Neiges d'Antan exudes a special warmth reflecting the soul of its proprietors. For generations, the timber and stone walls of this historic chalet have been cared for by the Bich family—a people dedicated to preserving the traditional alpine way of life.

Villa Principessa Elisa

Ristorante Gazebo
SS. del Brennero, 1616
55050 Massa Pisana-Lucca
Italy
Phone: 39 583 37 97 37
Chef Antonio Sanna

This graceful villa tucked away in the hills of Lucca, is one of Tuscany's most prestigious hotels. The architecture, interior design, and cuisine portray a harmonic blend of classic country and refined cosmopolitan luxury.

The medieval towers of Siena, Italy, etch an indelible image of the town's skyline into the memory of those who visit.

FRANCE

Château de Bagnolet

16101 Cognac
France
Not open to public—Contact Hennessy Cognac
Phone: 33 45 35 72 72
Chef Michel Dupont

Until thirty years ago, Chateau de Bagnolet was home to Cognac's first family—the Hennessys. Built in 1840, the unique chateau features an architectural style more in fitting with *Gone with the Wind* than traditional French designs. The bright and airy plantation-style house is surrounded by exotic tropical plants and lemon trees.

Château de la Messardière

Route de Tahiti
83990 St. Tropez
France
Phone: 33 94 56 76 00
Chef Jean-Louis Vosgien

This whimsical turn of the century palace is situated high on a hill in picturesque St. Tropez. Classic French furnishings embellish guest rooms while the dining area boasts sweeping views of the French Riviera.

Château de Locguenole

Route de Port-Louis
56700 Hennebont
France
Phone: 33 97 76 29 04
Chef Marc Angelle

Bordering the Bay of Biscay on Brittany's rugged, windy coast, this former castle rests in a perfect landscape of sea and forest. Inside, the atmosphere depicts the spectacular 19th century palace it once was.

Domaine de Valmouriane

Petite Route des Baux (D27)
13210 St. Remy de Provence
France
Phone: 33 90 92 44 62
Chef Stephane Bettinelli

Domaine de Valmouriane boasts a unique history. The main building was long inhabited by local Provençal shepherds, their families, and even their sheep. Today, the country inn is modernized but retains its special link to the past.

La Bastide de Moustiers

La Grisolière
04360 Moustiers-Ste.-Marie
France
Phone: 33 92 74 62 40
Chef Sonja Lee

In 17th century Provence, this charming farmhouse belonged to a well respected local cook. According to legend, when this French cuisinière died, she left behind this cozy home as well as a stack of valuable recipes. World-renowned Chef Alain Ducasse brought this long-dormant treasure to life and created an authentic atmosphere to savor the flavors of this colorful region.

La Chapelle Saint-Martin

Par Nieul
87510 Pres-Limoges
France
Phone: 33 55 75 80 17
Chef Gilles Dudognon

Parks, ponds, and rolling hills surround this country estate in Western France. Located near the famous village of Limoges, this 19th century squire's hall is adorned in its share of the fine porcelain that has been produced here for generations.

Le Goyen

Place Jean Simon
29770 Audierne
France
Phone: 33 98 70 08 88
Chef Dominique Quay

Basking in the cool breezes of Brittany's mystical Audierne Bay, Le Goyen reflects this wind-swept region's unique qualities. Decorated with maritime maps and overlooking the adjacent fishing port, the spirit of the sea is the overwhelming theme of this coastal inn.

Le Grand Vefour

17 Rue Beaujolais
75001 Paris
France
Phone: 33 1 42 96 56 27
Chef Guy Martin

Straight from the archives of French history, this award-winning restaurant dates back to the reign of Louis XV, who was king when the eatery opened in 1760. Facing the Palais-Royal gardens, Le Grand Vefour's premier location was a central arena for Parisians and visitors—and still is today.

Le Manoir du Lys

Croix Gauthier
Route de Juvigny
61140 Bagnoles-de-l'Orne
France
Phone: 33 33 37 80 69
Chef Franck Quinton

Normandy's green pastures and apple orchards lead to this peaceful country house, where traditional Norman meals are served and tranquility abounds.

Le Moulin de l'Abbaye

1 Route de Bourdeilles
24310 Brantome
France
Phone: 33 53 05 80 22
Chef Guy Guenego

This 12th-century mill was discovered and brought back to life by Regis Bulot—president of Relais and Chateaux. Today, the cozy inn overlooks a unique 16th century stone bridge and an old monk's garden. Inside, soft bright fabrics reflect the natural beauty that is the backdrop to this medieval French sanctuary.

Le Parc Victor Hugo

55/57 Avenue Raymond-Poincare
75116 Paris
France
Phone: 33 1 44 05 66 66
Chef Gilles Renault

A beautiful outdoor courtyard is the centerpiece to this elegant Paris hotel, comfortably decorated in British Colonial style. Although central to all of the city's wonderful eating establishments, the Victor Hugo has its own culinary claim-to-fame—the celebrated Le Relais du Parc Restaurant.

Marignan-Elysees

La Table du Marche Restaurant
12 Rue Marignan
75008 Paris
France
Phone: 33 1 40 76 34 56
Chef Christophe Leroy

Within walking distance to the famous Champs Elysées, this grand Parisian hotel is decked out in modern-art paintings and streamlined furniture. Although angled toward contemporary design, the hotel holds to tradition with La Table du Marche, an acclaimed restaurant serving fine French cuisine.

Royal Riviera

3 Avenue Jean Monnet
06230 St.-Jean-Cap-Ferrat
France
Phone: 33 93 01 20 20
Chef Yves Merville

Located in the historic fishing village of Saint-Jean-Cap-Ferrat, this luxury hotel remains true to its name. Awe-inspiring views of the French Riviera and the warm Mediterranean breeze attract visitors seeking a taste of Southern France.

Troisgros

Place Jean Troisgros
42300 Roanne
France
Phone: 33 77 71 66 97
Chef Michel Troisgros

Winner of three Michelin stars, Michel Troisgros is one of France's premier chefs. With his father, Pierre, the Troisgros team prepares extraordinary cuisine for guests of their world-renowned restaurant near Lyon.

Index